the
white
house

First published by O Books, 2008
O Books is an imprint of John Hunt Publishing Ltd., The Bothy, Deershot Lodge, Park Lane, Ropley,
Hants, SO24 0BE, UK
office1@o-books.net
www.o-books.net

Distribution in:	South Africa
	Alternative Books
UK and Europe	altbook@peterhyde.co.za
Orca Book Services	Tel: 021 555 4027 Fax: 021 447 1430
orders@orcabookservices.co.uk	
Tel: 01202 665432 Fax: 01202 666219	Text copyright Peter Pelz & Donald Reeves 2008
Int. code (44)	
	Design: Stuart Davies
USA and Canada	
NBN	ISBN: 978 1 84694 141 2
custserv@nbnbooks.com	
Tel: 1 800 462 6420 Fax: 1 800 338 4550	All rights reserved. Except for brief quotations in
	critical articles or reviews, no part of this book
Australia and New Zealand	may be reproduced in any manner without prior
Brumby Books	written permission from the publishers.
sales@brumbybooks.com.au	
Tel: 61 3 9761 5535 Fax: 61 3 9761 7095	The rights of Peter Pelz & Donald Reeves as
	author have been asserted in accordance with
Far East (offices in Singapore, Thailand,	the Copyright, Designs and Patents Act 1988.
Hong Kong, Taiwan)	
Pansing Distribution Pte Ltd	
kemal@pansing.com	A CIP catalogue record for this book is available
Tel: 65 6319 9939 Fax: 65 6462 5761	from the British Library.

Printed and Bound by Digital Book Print Ltd
www.digitalbookprint.com

O Books operates a distinctive and ethical publishing philosophy in
all areas of its business, from its global network of authors to
production and worldwide distribution.
This book is produced on FSC certified stock, within ISO14001
standards. The printer plants sufficient trees each year through
the Woodland Trust to absorb the level of emitted carbon in
its production.

the
white
house

Peter Pelz
& Donald Reeves

BOOKS

Winchester, UK
Washington, USA

CONTENTS

THE SOUL OF EUROPE

DEDICATION

We dedicate this book to Anel Alisic, Zoran Djukic, our advisors
and helpers, Emir Muhic, our translator, and Misha Stojnic,
our driver.

INTRODUCTION

GRAHAM DAY

Former Deputy High Representative and Head of Office,
Banja Luka,
Republika Srpska, Bosnia, 2003 - 2006

I was in former Yugoslavia for much of the period covered by this book. At that time almost all the 'outsiders' could feel the same mixture of pathos and insane barbarity which is recorded here. To fit one's own experience all one had to do was to change the location, time and family names concerned. Even though it deals only with one specific area, to me this book is valuable on two levels: it is important because it stands as testimony, not simply against those named for the horrors of that time and place, but also against all those 'outsiders' who knew and did nothing or made excuses for inaction.

The white house is a simple non-descript building which amply demonstrates the banality of horror. It speaks, however, to a lot more than that, during the recent war all over Bosnia and Herzegovina (BiH), schools, factories even grain silos were used as extempore places of detention. Within all places of detention atrocities took place. No one ethnic group was any more criminally insane than any other, but opportunity was unevenly divided and hence there is an asymmetry in the number of victims by ethnic group. As we have seen today in Iraq, victories provide a sometimes irresistible opportunity to commit atrocities.

During the war in BiH approximately a hundred thousand people died; the great majority of them civilians. Within this number approximately seventy thousand were Muslims who in the 1991 census were 44% of the population; approximately twenty thousand were Serbs who were approximately 31% of the population and about ten thousand Croats and others who were 25% of the population. These numbers for victims are being constantly refined but as of 2006 the order of magnitude is fixed. Many inside BiH wish to dispute these figures, those who claim more must produce compelling evidence that even more victims exist. Time and again they simply cannot do it except by bizarre double counting. Some wish to say that these numbers are too big; they fall in the same category as holocaust deniers, subjectively convinced but objectively completely out gunned by the growing weight of empirical evidence. Here I should acknowledge the pioneering work of the Research and Documentation Center in Sarajevo which of all the myriad agencies playing with this kind of numbers post war has consistently lead the way in informed and scholarly methodology. They have been a clear and consistent light in an otherwise dark place.

The Muslim community has the grievance of bearing many more victims proportionately than their pre war census figures would indicate. Sadly they have also been the loudest in decrying the figure of only a hundred thousand deaths, many of them clinging to the wartime propaganda figure of two hundred and fifty thousand dead. This puts me in mind of the riposte given by the former President Izetbegovic when accused that the Muslims in Sarajevo had deliberately bombed themselves in order to force the international community to act. He is supposed to have replied in an exasperated voice: "The international community has stood by and watched ten thousand Muslims die here in Sarajevo, why should the death of sixty more force them to act? Similarly, why make exaggerated claims for two hundred and fifty thousand deaths in a war when a hundred thousand can be proved. Are a hundred thousand not enough?"

Conversely the Serb community has had its share of either those who wish to deny the atrocities or to equate them to the many pogroms and massacres of World War Two. Both these reactions while human are essentially simply making more trouble for the future. Deniers are fortunately being slowly whittled down as the accumulating weight of empirical evidence makes denial more an act of deep personal trauma than any kind of defensible position. The equivalency arguments are essentially about revenge for former grievance. Revenge faces the time old problem of how much is enough? And where does it stop? Can a grandson really be held accountable for the crimes of the grandfather? I sincerely hope not.

There is not a lot of comment about the Croats in this book because from a demographic point of view in north-west Bosnia they were essentially by far the smallest community. During the war and subsequently they have been lead by a spiritual leader Bishop Komarica, who is acknowledged in the book. The bishop has been loud in condemning the International Community for not doing more to bring the small but important Croat Community back to North West BiH. It is, however, sadly true that most of this community who left have been given better prospects in neighbouring Croatia and will never return permanently.

These simple facts in themselves should start to caution the casual observer about drawing hasty conclusions about the Bosnian conflict. There are no simple answers to even apparently simple questions such as: was this a civil war? Answer: yes and no. Was this a war of aggression? Answer: yes and no. Were there understandable historical root causes and hence some form of twisted justification of this violence? Answer: yes and no. Who then was responsible for the war? (A case can be made for blaming both Stalin and Tito whose unmistakable historical legacies drove certain key individuals and institutions). These questions continue to swirl around today in Bosnia, with the paradoxical and ambiguous answers clouding politics and traumatizing families.

In each community in Bosnia historical grievances are maintained over the generations. In the 1960s and 70s the urbane and sophisticated city Yugoslavs appeared to have broken away from this essentially peasant phenomenon. Some succeeded, but within the leadership cadre of each community there were experts at resurrecting and enflaming these historical grievances. In World War Two there had been vicious pogroms of Yugoslav against Yugoslav. These were remembered. Tito had suppressed certain areas and groups; this was remembered. The communist party had suppressed religion of all forms and this was remembered. There was no need for any individual to cling to one chosen trauma when a veritable smorgasbord of trauma was on offer in only the last fifty years.

The single most important residual issue of the deaths during the war is the fact that in 2006 there are approximately eighteen thousand persons still unaccounted for. It is beyond reason to suggest that these missing persons are anything other than dead; yet loved ones and family have no body and no closure of the trauma. This would be a tragic enough event for the individuals concerned but in the context of deeply fractured BiH it is a political issue as well. In each election fiery rhetoric about missing persons is used to inflame passions on all sides, to the misery of the victims' families and general detriment of BiH as a struggling emerging state. In the book you will meet people who know the whereabouts of many of these bodies but will not come forward. This grievance alone if unresolved is a seed of future conflict.

Approximately two million people were driven or fled from their homes (half the population). Ten years after the war ended we can now see that there has been an historic population shift and that most of the two million are not back in their pre war homes. The reasons for not returning are much more complicated than just fear of return, but they surely would not have left in the way that they did without being driven by fear. This fact of displacement on the ground has prolonged the ugly and potentially conflictive, post war trauma, as it does in every incidence of partition, a fact often glossed over by real-politik partition advocates.

Why is this important context for *the white house*? About thirty thousand people were driven from their homes in the Priedor region of BiH during the war. Three thousand were detained and approximately one thousand bodies remain unaccounted for. *The white house* as a book is a micro-cosm of the war. The war was about ethnic cleansing. It was a war to delineate territory which could from then on be 'living space' for one ethnic group or the other. Ethnic cleansing was not an accidental bi-product; it was an aim or objective in itself. Populations are made to move by fear, it is the rational use of terror. *The white house* describes a present day manifestation of the rational use of terror.

Where can BiH go from here? Books like *the white house* point the way without polemic or prejudice. First the people of BiH must get together and talk. They must admit the truth about what happened village by village. They need a people's history. NGOs like the Research and Documentation Agency have already gathered much of the raw data. Books like *the white house* have pioneered the way. What is needed now is a national dialogue, national truth telling and where possible national forgiveness. Where forgiveness is not possible, and this is quite often the case, then national public acceptance of the right of the other community to existence in dignity and safety.

Patterns of repeated violent conflict all over the world require the root causes to be addressed. The key to starting this process is the truth. The truth is never enough just in itself but it is an unavoidable first step. Without the truth, there can be no dialogue, no trust and no possibility of a future. The path to eventual reconciliation after violent conflict is always generations not just decades. It requires the truth to be accepted by all sides and then a dialogue of understanding and getting to know the 'other'.

The white house can be a small first step in the direction of reconciliation if the people of BiH and more particularly North West BiH want it to be.

ACKNOWLEDGEMENTS

The Soul of Europe would like to thank the present owners of the mine. It was they who invited and paid us to bring together Bosnian Serbs and Bosnian Muslims in the dispute about a memorial to those who lost their lives in Omarska.

We owe a special thanks to Kemal Pervanic, *The Killing Days* (Blake Publishing) and to Rezak Hukanovic, *The Tenth Circle of Hell* (Little Brown Book Group).

We would like to thank Anel Alisic, Andrew Barr, Kate Goslett, Dan Gretton, John Paul Lederach, Bishop Holloway, Simon Goodenough, and Jeremy Seabrook for their sustained encouragment and friendly criticism.

We thank John Hunt, publisher of 'O' books for his patience and advice.

We drew on the considerable wisdom and experience of Graham Day, the Former Deputy High Representative and Head of Office, Banja Luka, Republika Srpska. We consulted him at every stage and we are grateful to him for his solidarity with the Soul of Europe.

We have omitted the names of the participants employed by the mine. The present owners acquired the mine in 2004. The events described in this book took place under different management in 1992.

Boris Danovic is a pseudonym for the former mine manager who became a significant participant of the process.

The main body of the book was written by Peter Pelz. Donald Reeves wrote the Foreword and Afterword.

We have tried to be as accurate as possible. If there are any inaccuracies, they are unintended and the fault is ours and ours alone.

FOREWORD

In April 2004 a new mining company acquired the iron ore mine at Omarska, near Prijedor in north western Bosnia. The acquisition was part of the company's policy to buy up and then invest in dilapidated state owned mines in central and southeastern Europe.

Omarska (1) was used as a killing camp from May to August 1992 during the Bosnia War. Bosniaks (2) and Croats had been brought to the camp to be exterminated.

The new mine owners' acquisition provoked demands from the survivors of Omarska for a memorial to be established in the mine complex.

It was realized that if these demands were not met the region could be destabilized and this could harm the mine's potential profitability. Survivors demanded a memorial. Serb management and mine workers would have none of it.

The Soul of Europe (3) was commissioned to bring Serbs, Bosniaks and Croats together to agree on a proposal for a memorial.

We were invited because we had demonstrated it was possible to gather together former adversaries in Bosnia. In 2001, at our invitation, senior politicians, religious leaders and business people from Banja Luka, the administrative centre of the Republika Srpska, together with the mayor of Banja Luka and his cabinet, traveled to the International Centre for Reconciliation at Coventry Cathedral for four days of intensive discussion. Our success had been noted in Bosnia by the international community.

Though this be madness yet there is method in it
Hamlet, William Shakespeare

'Many witnesses speak of good inter-communal relations, of friendships across ethnic and coincident religious divides, of inter-marriages and of generally harmonious relations', write the judges of the ICTY (International Criminal Tribunal for Former

Yugoslavia) in the trial of Dusko Tadic, the first individual from Prijedor to have been tried and sentenced at The Hague for 'acts of persecution, murder and inhuman treatment committed in 1992 against Bosniaks at Omarska.'

Those witnesses were referring to life at Prijedor in the 1980s.

But on April 30th 1992 life changed there for ever. A meticulous program of ethnic cleansing began. For six months a group of Serbs, known as the 'Crisis Staff' had been preparing for this day. Non-Serbs were sacked. Bank accounts were frozen. Bosniak leaders and professional people in Prijedor were rounded up and taken to Omarska: teachers, lawyers, shopkeepers, religious leaders, accountants, local politicians and officials. Travel within Prijedor was almost impossible. Communication with the outside world was suspended. Following an incident when two Serbs were killed, all non-Serbs were required to wear white arm bands and display white flags. In all, forty three thousand people, all non-Serbs – and about half of the population fled, disappeared or were driven into exile or taken to Omarska and other camps to be tortured and killed. The precise number of those who died is still unknown, but there were certainly more than three thousand and less than four thousand.

The purpose of this barbarism was to create a pure and greater Serbia. It was orchestrated from Belgrade and was the major political impulse behind the war in Croatia and Bosnia. Western governments, initially, were reluctant to intervene, giving the excuse that these conflicts were merely stirring up ancient tribal hatreds. Serbs often told us: 'This was a civil war.' We firmly contradicted them.

When the war finally came to an end in December 1995, Bosnia was divided into two entities, the mainly Bosnia/Croat entity whose capital is Sarajevo, and the Republika Srspka, the predominantly Serb entity, whose administrative centre is Banja Luka. The Republika Srspka had been proclaimed in January 1992, but the Dayton Accord did not allow it to have the status of an independent state. But both entities had the trappings of independence: presidents, prime ministers, various ministries, separate flags, different national anthems and coats of arms.

The international community required the entities to work together to create a modern European state. Under their constant pressure a structure has been created for a single police force, a joint army, a state border and customs service, a single judiciary and much more. But there is a marked reluctance by Bosnian politicians of all the ethnic groups to inhabit the structure, because of the enduring strength of nationalism on all sides.

Prijedor, the second city after Banja Luka in the Republika Srpska, received special attention from the United Nations and a range of international agencies to encourage the return of those driven from their homes. Prijedor is geographically closer to the Federation while Srebrenica, for example, is close to Serbia. Moreover, the Bosniak villages and settlements around Prijedor had long been homogeneous. Better to return to a ruined village and rebuild there than to return to an ethnically mixed area. Some of the Bosniaks and survivors of Omarska whom we would meet in the following pages were returnees to these villages. Twenty thousand are said to have returned, but the figure is now lower. There was no attempt by the UN and its satellites to integrate the returnees into Serb Prijedor. Intimidation, discrimination and a completely inadequate school system led many to leave. Certainly driving through some of these villages in an early winter evening is to be struck by the darkness, little if any street lighting and most houses standing empty.

This broad perspective omits one significant factor: the mistrust and suspicion that many Bosnians, especially public figures and officials had for 'westerners'. Five years in Bosnia had prepared us for this. Serbs believe the West want to demolish the entities, so the Republika Srpska would cease to exist (and with it their identity as Serbs). Bosniaks feel betrayed by the West for not preventing the massacre at Srebrenica and failing to capture Radovan Karadjic and General Mladic. The Croats, the smallest ethnic group in Bosnia, feel ignored and marginalized.

Moreover as we learnt from many Bosnian friends, there was palpable anger at the swarms of NGOs and agencies, large and small, which parachuted into Bosnia after the end of the war. Indiscriminate interaction, far from being welcomed, was often interpreted as a lack of respect.

Therefore as well as trying to bring Serbs, Bosniaks and Croats together, we had to convince them of our commitment to being of use. We were like a ground bass. If the note sounded firm and clear, then their trust in us as mediators could develop, and the discordant notes had some possibilities of resolution.

In this we did have some success. After an early meeting with Serb and Bosniak women, one of them, a Serb manager at the mine headquarters, thanked us for coming: 'You show human qualities; and you keep on coming back.' Six months later after a difficult meeting, noticing the look of anxiety on our faces, she asked: 'Why are you looking so sad?' I replied: 'I was not sure if we had done enough, and if we should have done more.' She put her hand on my arm encouragingly and said: 'It will be all right. You'll see. It will be all right.'

We devised a plan. We had to discover if any Serbs, Bosniaks and Croats would be ready to meet and engage in serious conversations about the past. Finding this was indeed so, we then gathered people together and finally set up meetings for Bosniaks and Serbs to develop plans for the memorial. These were presented at a conference in Banja Luka in December 2005 before the local and international media. From April 2005 to February 2006 the Soul of Europe spent half of every month in Prijedor.

There is now a mass of expertise and wisdom in mediation, conflict resolution and processes of reconciliation, some of which we drew on (4). Practitioners and academics produce a steady flow of sophisticated approaches to facilitation, negotiation and all manner of group work.

But at its heart the road towards reconciliation is a long, hard and profoundly human activity. These are not always realized by techniques, although they can help. And the journey never ends. It is never completed. Politics and history are not like that. There is always more to be done. But without reconciliation, even partial reconciliation, there is descent into barbarism and never-ending violence.

So from our experience we knew we had to be ready to hear the raw memories of Bosniaks and Serbs (Croats had mostly left the area, so they hardly figure in our story). We knew we would need to be patient and to listen well. We knew humility would be required of us, for we were after all visitors in a country not our own. We realized we would need all our own wisdom to interpret what we were being told. We had to be alert, so nothing was missed. We knew we would have to be prepared to take risks, that the outcome of tense and awkward meetings might be unpredictable. We knew from the day we arrived in Prijedor that there would no short cuts, no quick fixes and no instant solutions.

This is the story of what happened.

NOTES

1) For more information about the Prijedor region during the Bosnia War:

    a. The Prijedor Report – final report of the United Nations Commission of Experts. S/1994/674/Add.2 (Voume 1)

    b. *Raw Memory – Prijedor, Laboratory of Ethnic Cleansing* by Isabelle Wesselingh and Arnaud Vaulerin, Saqi Books. ISBN 086356528X

2) BOSNIAK – Bosnian Muslims are invariably described as Bosniaks, in order to separate their identity from religion. The work Bosniak means Bosnian and was once used for all inhabitants of Bosnia, regardless of faith. The other main ethnic groups in Bosnia are Serbs (Orthodox Christian) and Croats (Catholics).

3) THE SOUL OF EUROPE – see www.soulofeurope.org
For the memorial project we had a team of six. This was made up of two project managers: Anel Alisic (Bosniak) and Zoran Djukic (Serb Croat), an interpreter, Emir Muhic (Bosniak), a driver, Misha Stojnic (Serb), Peter Pelz and Donald Reeves, directors of the Soul

of Europe. Kate Goslett, psychotherapist and chair of the Soul of Europe's Advisory Council, joined the team for one visit.

4) The writings of John Paul Lederach, Professor of International Peacebuilding at the Joan B Kroc Institute of International Peace Studies at Notre Dame University, particularly *The Moral Imagination*, Oxford University Press 2005 ISBN 0-19-517454-2

Democracy and Deep Rooted Conflict: Options for Negotiations, published by the International Institute for Democracy and Electoral Assistance. ISBN 91-89098-22-6. A most useful handbook.

The Moral Imagination by Donald Reeves, available on the Soul of Europe's website. This lecture given at Lambeth Palace in May 2006 is a reflection on the Omarska project, incorporating the insights of John Paul Lederach.

DRAMATIS PERSONAE
PRIJEDOR
SURVIVORS

Kemal Pervanic	Author, survivor of Omarska, living in England
Kasim Pervanic	Survivor of Omarska, living in Kevljane
Rezak Hukanovic	Author, survivor of Omarska
Mirsad Duratovic	Community leader, survivor of Omarska
Nusreta Sivac	Judge, survivor of Omarska
Muharem Murselovic	Local and National Deputy, survivor of Omarska
Mirsad Islamovic	Councillor, survivor of Omarska
Sadko Mujagic	Survivor of Omarska, living in Rotterdam
Emsuda Mujagic	Director of the Kozarac Peace Centre
Dr Azra Pasalic	Doctor and Speaker of the Municipal Assembly
Mirjana Vehabovic	Croat delegate of the Council of People
Seida Karabasic	Izvor, organization for missing persons
Edin Ramulic	Izvor, organization for missing persons
Jasmina Devic	Bridges for Peace, organization of women survivors

THE MUNICIPALITY

Marko Pavic	Mayor of Prijedor
Biljana Malbasic	Financial Advisor to the mayor.
Dusan Tubin	Chairman of the mayor's cabinet
Mladen Grahovac	Engineer, member of SDP, Social Democratic Party
Zarko Gvozden	Member of the SDP, Social Democratic Party
Jeff Ford	Head of Office in Prijedor, Organization for Security and Cooperation in Europe, OSCE

THE 'ROUND TABLE'

Katerina Panic	Journalist, SRNA (Srpska Republic News) Agency
Vedran Grahovac	Post graduate student of Philosophy
Aleksander (Sasha) Drakulic	Journalist ESPRIT Radio
Tijana Glusac	Student, Philosophy Faculty Banja Luka
Zoran Ergerac	Marketing Consultant
Nino Jauz	Councillor, Alliance of Independent Social Democrats SNDP

BANJA LUKA

Graham Day	Office of the High Representative in Banja Luka
Giorgio Blais	Director of OSCE Regional Centre in Banja Luka
Bishop Franjo Komarica	Catholic Bishop of Banja Luka
Vladika Jefrem	Orthodox Bishop of Banja Luka

THE OMARSKA PROJECT TEAM

Anel Alisic	Project Manager
Zoran Djukic	Project Manager
Emir Muhic	Interpreter
Misha Stojnic	Driver
Kate Goslett	Consultant to the Soul of Europe

| Donald Reeves | Director of the Soul of Europe |
| Peter Pelz | Director of the Soul of Europe |

the white house

FROM FEAR TO A HANDSHAKE

SILENCE

The white house stood at the edge of a field, visible through a gap between a large hangar on the right and the Omarska mine administration offices on the left. Though dwarfed by the rest of the mine, this shed managed to focus attention on its ordinariness. It looked sinister, set apart, perhaps because we knew its history, perhaps because everyone else averted their eyes.

Before the war a former mine director had the shed built as a shelter from rain for workers. After the war it became a canteen.

During the war for four months in 1992, May to August, hottest time of the year in Bosnia, the white house became a human abattoir. As part of Serb policy of ethnic cleansing, killing Bosniaks and Croats throughout the region (up to four thousand), thugs humiliated, tortured and murdered hundreds in the conveniently isolated mine of Omarska, about ten miles from the nearest large town, Prijedor. At Omarska these activities could take place in relative secrecy. Though atrocities were perpetrated in all the mine buildings, torture and murder happened mostly in the white house.

Had international journalists not discovered the killings at Omarska and shocked the world with images reminding people of Nazi concentration camps, the white house would have continued operating to the end of the war three years later. So the journalists saved thousands of lives. International pressure forced the closure of the mine, as well as Trnopolje, the nearby holding camp for women, who were raped by local police and passing soldiers, and a third killing centre, Keraterm, a tile factory on the outskirts of Prijedor. The four months of Omarska's existence as a killing camp in 1992 witnessed the worst atrocities in Europe since the Second World War. That same year I happened to be travelling through

Austria, just a few hours drive away, unaware of the horrors being perpetrated at this isolated mine in Northern Bosnia.

The recently appointed mine manager drove us round the mine, showing us the massive crater in which heavy machinery and match-stick men crawled over distant mounds of rock streaked with iron ore. It seemed unlikely, though not impossible, that still missing bodies could be buried there. Mass graves were being found outside the mine. The mine manager showed us round the hangar where the same large metal hooks hung on which victims had been tortured and killed, and the office buildings where the same rooms were being used by administrative staff in which victims, men and women, had been interrogated and also tortured, raped and killed. We stared through the windows of the white house itself, a locked shed, noting the dust, a chair knocked over on the floor and for some reason an old television set on an otherwise empty stack of shelves. Nothing in this characterless and neglected place spoke of the atrocities that had been committed there.

Afterwards we sat in the canteen surrounded by taciturn workers finishing their lunch.

'What needs to be done with the white house?' we asked the chief engineer, much to the mine manager's consternation.

The chief engineer responded amicably, but mournfully, aware of the situation: 'Something has to be done.'

The mine manager meanwhile chatted with some of the other workers through his translator assistant, a large young man, his blank face as unrevealing as the white house itself.

I looked at the workers, a poor rough lot, suspicious of strangers, and wondered whether any of them had taken part in the tortures and murders. During the summer of 1992 workers had driven the bodies to be dumped outside the mine where they would not easily be found.

The mine manager, his kindly smiling driver and the expressionless translator assistant drove us in the boss's black Audi to some of these places.

First we looked at a large lake outside the mine of Omarska

where the pastoral beauty of lapping water, orchards and hills in the background took our attention away from the disquieting thought that bodies could have been thrown into the deeper parts. The translator became momentarily animated, rhapsodising over the sun-drenched landscape, announcing he could live no-where else in the world. The more business-minded mine manager enthused about new plans for expanding the mine, pointing at the nearby villages and farms which had already been marked for removal to make way for another massive crater.

Then the black Audi bumped its way along miles of dirt tracks through the sprawling remains of the Bosniak village of Kevljane where all the houses had been burnt and the inhabitants either fled or were taken to Omarska and only few survived. Some of these survivors were now returning to rebuild their homes, next to Serb neighbours who resented their presence. What had the war been about if not to get rid of these unwanted people? We reached the edge of the village where an elderly Bosniak couple, eyes sparkling with pleasure at meeting strangers, smilingly pointed the way to a nearby meadow. Earlier a Serb had shrugged his shoulders and turned away, pretending not to know. Just two months previous to our visit a mass grave in this meadow revealed four hundred and fifty bodies of men, women and children, shot or beaten to death.

The bodies had been taken for identification to a large warehouse in Sejkovac, near the Bosniak town of Sanski Most, across the border between the two entities of Bosnia.

Bulldozers had flattened the meadow and we gazed across the expanse of mud, weeds and grass to some distant woods, trying to picture the mass of bones and skulls piling up. The mine manager, told us of his shock at what he saw, apparently not having known anything about the ethnic cleansing when he came to begin the task of making the mine profitable. Looking at the scale of the burial he realized that mine machinery must have been used to transport the bodies.

The black Audi slowly negotiated further miles of muddy track then speeded smoothly along the road to Prijedor and beyond to the acres of deserted iron-ore excavation at Ljubija, site of the largest mine in the region which had once employed five thousand workers. A couple of guards reluctantly but obediently opened the gates to the boss. Mass graves had already been located in this large derelict unused area where mounds, disused pits and especially several lakes provided convenient locations for hiding large quantities of bodies.

We drove past rusting machinery, along gravel roads winding through hilly scrubland, and almost collided with a van driven by two startled locals who then speeded noisily towards the exit. The translator and the driver stayed in the Audi while we stood with the mine manager on a rock overlooking a deep lake below, and listened to him explaining how this mine had been exhausted, but the new owners had agreed to take responsibility for the machinery. I walked for a while on my own and looking over the lake noticed a woman's pink and blue shawl caught in a bush by the water's edge.

We encountered no suspicious guards or surprised locals at our final destination of the day, the bleak expanse of another disused mine, Tomasica, where huge cranes and containers rusted on flat weed-strewn stony meadows. Here bodies were known to be buried, but no one was yet prepared to say where. Those who knew waited for advantage or reward.

Meanwhile the bodies from the mass grave at Kevljane were added to others mounting up in a warehouse at Sejkovac by the River Sana outside Sanski Most, remains needing identification. Since whole families had been killed, not even DNA testing could help tell who all these people were. Many of them would remain forever nameless and forgotten.

Skulls, arm and leg bones lay in heaps on trestle tables while upwards of a thousand heaps of individual remains, including the tiny skeletons of babies, were stacked in plastic bags, one on top of each other against the walls, or carefully laid out in rows on the large cool floor of the warehouse. Scraps of clothing, shoes, bags and other personal possessions were placed in tidy heaps on top of the dismembered skeletons. These indications of private existences were poignant evidence that the victims did not die natural deaths but had been murdered.

Looking closer we noted the injuries suffered, the bullet holes in the skulls, and the fractured bones of those beaten to death. Mustiness mingled with a sulphurous odour.

Silence reigned here as in a sacred place. Several assistants in the process of sorting and identification observed us mournfully.

THE LONG HOUSE

Calm flows the Sana
Past the long house beyond a roadside café.
One thousand bodies lie on the floor
Reduced to bones, bits of spine and crumbling cracked skulls.
No one knows yet who they are.
Women wail for missing husbands and children:
'Where are you, my husband, my son? Where are you my love?'
Calm flows the Sana
Past flowerful meadows, hills and woods
Past Misha's childhood home, past Anel's auntie's house.
Past an old man with his scythe.
'Where are you, my husband, my son?'
Calm flows the Sana
Past the monastery on the hill.
Nationalist flags flutter over the chapel
('Religion has nothing do with politics,' the bishop said).
Calm flows the Sana

THE ROAD TO OMARSKA
MEETING KEMAL PERVANIC

Before taking on this work we had to meet Kemal Pervanic, a survivor of the Omarska killing camp and author of *The Killing Days*. We needed to find out whether he approved of our part in the project. If he insisted on us not being involved we would have turned the work down.

Another survivor, Rezak Hukanovic's *The Tenth Circle of Hell*, focuses on the violence, especially gruelling the account of his torture in the white house itself. Kemal Pervanic's book describes the panic in the days preceding imprisonment, the struggle to survive day after terrifying day in Omarska and eventual liberation. The end of the book hints at the many years it took to recover from the trauma. Kemal avoids descriptions of actual violence he did not see, but reports the consequences he witnessed, the screams he heard, the callous behaviour of Serb guards, several of whom had been his school friends, the suffering and deaths of his fellow prisoners. His book evokes palpable terror. He gives a meticulous account of the outbreak of war, rumours of the steadily approaching Serb army burning villages, shooting on sight, communities of unarmed men, women and children hiding under bridges, in the rivers or surrounding woods, knowing they were unprotected, forgotten by the rest of the world, and waiting for their inevitable fate. The book's opening pages create universal empathy: we can all recognize ourselves and our neighbours in these ordinary people - and feel the gut-wrenching fear. The rest of the book takes us into a territory of such cruelty and suffering none of us can even begin to guess at, and begs the question: how would we have survived?

Kemal Pervanic stood waif-like on Folkestone station, gaze bleached, a reed bent by a tempest and trying to grow upright again. The asceticism of his austere features, accentuated by long hair swept back tightly and tied into a ponytail, made him look like an Orthodox monk, a stark reminder of the close interlinking of religions and ethnic groups in Bosnia, all the same nationality. The extremity of his experience endowed him with authority. We listened. Like the survivors of Auschwitz in Claude Lanzmann's *Shoah*, Kemal possessed a calm, transcendent quality, shared by those who have passed through the holocaust. They are able to speak of reconciliation and forgiveness in a way denied those who did not endure what they suffered. But the trauma does not go away, and for all the therapy and counselling, there can be no closure for these people. They display a unique humanity; people who understand the pointlessness of revenge and have reached an understanding that for the world to carry on people have to learn to live together.

Kemal Pervanic spoke of his parents now refugees in Newcastle, mother stoical, father broken in spirit. Kemal's brother Kasim had returned to rebuild their home, whatever the difficulties and obstacles, determined to see the return of his family to Bosnia.

Kemal Pervanic played us a video of his recent visit home, the first time since he had been imprisoned in Omarska and then driven from his own country. The film shows him arriving at the border between Croatia and Bosnia, breaking down suddenly sobbing and being held by his wife, Lea. He picks his way through the rubble of home, looted and burnt, finding utensils and childhood toys scattered among the weeds of a long neglected garden. The silence as the camera follows him speaks of an ordinary life shattered, and leaves questions hanging unanswered as to why, what made people behave with such savagery and how we could stop it happening again.

Showing us documentaries about Omarska, Kemal frowned disapprovingly at the lies and exaggerations of fellow inmates. 'They could not possibly have seen this,' he commented as they spoke on camera of murderers kissing their victims and licking the blood. The depravity of what happened did not need embellishing.

After his reserved demeanour at Folkestone station, cautious and exhausted by so many concerned do-gooders and the need to continually repeat his story, he warmed to a tearful embrace by the time we left, stirred by the prospect of a memorial at Omarska. These emotions however opened the trauma once more. Later developments of the project disturbed him and he withdrew support.

On a stormy night, shortly before leaving for Bosnia, three nightmares one after the other woke me in a cold sweat. First I dreamt of a battle in thick woods, Serbs calling each other and shooting. For some reason I was sleeping on the forest floor, hiding in terror under my sheet. Then I dreamt of talking to a cheerful 'chetnik', name for a Serb soldier but who in my dream told me he was a Muslim. I felt an inexplicable intense bond between us. He told me about the need to know history and explained the machismo of Balkan males. With a sudden shock I realized he was Arkan, one of the most feared Serb warlords, assassinated in Belgrade six years earlier. Finally I dreamt of a large truck coming round the corner, and I hid under brushwood, knowing I would be killed if found.

ZITOMISLICE: AN ORTHODOX GATHERING

Before engaging with the significant people for the project, Bosniak survivors of Omarska and Serb workers in the mine, we seized a unique opportunity of meeting Serb political and religious leaders gathering together for the opening of a rebuilt Orthodox monastery at Zitomislice, not far from Mostar. We needed to gauge their reaction to the memorial and judge from it the scale of difficulties our mediation process might encounter. We also hoped our presence there might be reassuring for the Serbs in Prijedor.

After a sleepless night in Sarajevo, dogs barking to each other from different neighbourhoods until daybreak when the muezzin calls took over in more melodious form, we drove to Zitomislice and watched the mists rise from mountain ranges and the ravines of the River Neretva. We arrived at the monastery under a scorching May midday sun. Families picnicked under cherry trees and crowds pressed into the cramped courtyards of the monastery, eager to catch a glimpse of the now elderly and venerable Patriarch Pavle, well into his nineties, who had come from Belgrade.

Zitomislice represented a Serb outpost in the mainly Croat and Bosniak parts of western Bosnia, known as Herzegovina. During the recent war Orthodox Serbs were persecuted, killed and driven out of the region with the same ferocity as they persecuted Croats and Bosniaks in other parts of Bosnia. So the presence of the patriarch with as many Orthodox bishops as could be mustered, as well as a significant tally of Serb politicians, emphasised the triumph of the return of Orthodox Serbs to this part of the country where they had long been a weak and victimized minority. The next step would be the rebuilding of the Orthodox Cathedral in Mostar itself, a city divided ethnically between Croats and Bosniaks, each community on either side of the River Neretva, the rebuilt celebrated Mostar Bridge now shooting like an arrow over the deep chasm that separated the town physically and metaphorically. The Catholic Bishop Peric had constructed an extra tall tower for the Catholic cathedral, as well as a massive cross on the hillside overlooking the minarets and mosques bristling on the opposite bank of the river.

First the politicians arrived with their entourages of minders. Svetlana Cenic tugged our sleeves, wondering at our presence. Now Minister for Finance of the Republika Srpska, we had got to know her when she used to be economics advisor to the then vice-president, now President Dragan Cavic. Both had attended a consultation we organized in Coventry, September 2001, where we brought together Serb, Muslim and Croat political and religious leaders from Banja Luka to talk about reconciliation. The present Prime Minister Pero Bukejlovic, then minister for economic affairs, had spent boozy evenings with me at the consultation, stretching his legs, drinking whisky and discussing the art of rakija production. He solved the riddle puzzling me how pears got inside bottles of the potent brandy by explaining the bottles were placed over the ripening fruit, so I had this image of an orchard glinting with glass. We bonded over this joke, and the moment he saw me at Zitomislice immediately wanted to come over and hug me, but remembered the same instant that he was now prime minister and had to behave with dignity, so the warm smile immediately froze into a sad rictus.

Svetlana Cenic, in modest white, a contrast to her usual power-dressing in brightly coloured two-piece suits, the pallor of her skin emphasised by a mass of jet-black hair, had always been the brains behind the Republika Srprska government. She listened to our brief for the Omarska project, looking uncharacteristically ill at ease. 'Yes, they have a big problem and it needs sorting out,' she sighed resignedly, but relieved someone else was taking over responsibility. At least we hoped we could count on the politicians not obstructing us, even if they were unwilling to support a project which by its nature implicated them.

Patriarch Pavle arrived in a procession of elaborately robed and crowned bishops and priests, the crowd surging forward and being held back by cordons of armed police from the Federation. Rows of guns and nuns pressed against each other. Bishop Vasilje from Bjelajina made himself conspicuous, moving rapidly among the politicians, his black cassock flapping like a raven's wings, muttering conspiratorially to them as he ministered the sacrament and flashing ferocious glances in every direction. He was after all on enemy territory.

Bosniak President SulejmanTihic bravely attended the celebrations, his bald head perspiring unprotected under the afternoon sun as the crowds of Serbs booed his presence. We had got to know him well when he was deputy speaker of the National Assembly in Banja Luka, a lone Bosniak representative among enemies. Since then he had returned to Sarajevo to lead his party. Though recognizing and greeting us warmly, his eyes glanced constantly over our heads, scouting for ever-present dangers. He would of course support any memorial project for killed Bosniaks, but his comment about 'mining in a graveyard' alerted us to the difficulty of our task.

The politicians sat on rows of chairs stared at by crowds of locals, mostly farmers with their wives and ragamuffin children, while a troupe of girls in traditional Serb maiden costumes danced gravely and sang.

We met representatives of the organization which paid for the rebuilding of the monastery at a banquet in a local restaurant, smartly dressed executives of an ostensibly international Serb business who invited us to Belgrade. Later we learnt that their chief boss was a funder of Radovan Karadjic's bodyguards.

THE ELEPHANT IN THE ROOM

'Prijedor is a black hole,' Misha Stojnic our Serb driver told us as we left Sarajevo. 'The world wants to forget us.' It turned out his pithy analysis described the place only too accurately.

Misha Stojnic's life story echoed that of the majority of decent men and women throughout the former Yugoslavia who suddenly found themselves in a maelstrom of nationalist politics, war and ethnic cleansing. His candid face, eyes permanently round with sorrow and hurt, expressed perpetual disappointment at a life destroyed by circumstances beyond his ability to influence. This shy and polite man used to work in a Prijedor bank. Before that he had earned well in Switzerland as a 'gast-arbeiter', by willingly working long hours and saving enough money to marry and raise a family. The war closed the bank. The recent arrival of an international mining company to reopen Omarska at least enabled his wife to find work as a secretary at the mine head office in Prijedor, so they did not starve. Unemployed, except when asked to do the occasional driving job, Misha mostly sat at home reading the papers, talking to neighbours, kicking his feet and worrying how to care for his family, including two children, constantly needing materials for school and daily life. Balkan macho society considered it humiliating for the man of the house to be without income while the wife was the earner. Far worse than this shame, seared the knowledge that many of the major criminals and rich local politicians had been his school friends. They had played in the same basket-ball team, Misha being its most popular player, valued for his strategy skills and enthusiasm. Now these crooks lived luxurious lives in spacious country houses and posh town flats, surrounded by beautiful women and minders, driving expensive cars always smiling and waving at Misha in the street, but not helping him. Misha's story illustrates a bitter truth: ruthless, amoral entrepreneurs often flourish while decent, law-abiding citizens suffer and lose out.

Misha drove us through the mountains between Doboj and Banja Luka. Staring at the miles of deserted landscape, the conversations with Svetlana Cenic and SulejmanTihic began to alarm me and I even feared momentarily that Misha might be an assassin, sent by the local politicians to prevent us carrying out our work. I expected him to stop the car in a remote forest, order us to get out, shoot us in the head, then bury us somewhere we would never be found. Even at this first meeting it seemed absurd and offensive that I could suspect such a sweet-natured friendly man who spent the whole time he was our driver trying to please us.

However we immediately became aware of an elephant in the room. He talked about the privations of war, the despair of unemployment, the halving of the work-force at the mine and closure of the banks, but he avoided all mention of our project. The urgent issues of relations between ethnic groups, the killings and the need for memorials were ignored.

Our hotel in Banja Luka, the Atina, was known as the property of one of the town's big crooks. The then High Representative, Paddy Ashdown, stayed there on his visits to Banja Luka with his bodyguards. American embassy staff and guests refused to use the Atina even though it was hard to find any hotel, or business for that matter, in the town that did not have gangster connections. The Atina's gleaming marble floors and chrome-framed glass frontage displayed the ostentatious glamour of large amounts of money requiring quick spending. A gigantic plasma TV screen in the bar showed either the sports or MTV channels in constant rotation. However in contrast to this cold superficial gloss the attractive young staff turned out to be warm, polite and helpful, always opening doors, smiling, serving drinks and food with eager desire to please. A tip of-course encouraged this enthusiasm; earning about two hundred euros a month, even a regular five euro note slipped under a plate or in the hand, made a difference to these youngsters, who dreamed of emigrating.

We met Kemal Pervanic's brother, Kasim, to deliver money from Kemal for rebuilding the family home. In contrast to the conciliatory Kemal, Kasim was driven by bitterness and revenge. He had also survived Omarska, but unlike his more sensitive brother, had dared to observe the beatings and killings taking place, even at risk to his own life. For Kasim there were no good Serbs. Angry determination gave him strength to endure daily struggles to purchase materials, gain legal permissions and to simply survive the constant encounters with people who had once persecuted and tried to get rid of him. The thought of family, parents being able to return home, Kemal and his wife visiting, maybe even settling there and raising a family, gave purpose to his life that had been shattered not only by the war, but also a tragic relationship with a girlfriend in Germany who died of cancer. Kasim's dark eyes burnt with intense resolve, his strong, wiry physique like a bullet. No-one would be allowed to interfere with his life again. And if the Serbs wanted another war, he was ready to take them on.

The following day we visited the mines at Omarska, Ljubija and Tomasica meeting the mine management and workers in order to establish as substantial a rapport as possible with these people for the project. These Serbs clearly had no wish to be reminded of the past, and at this stage were adamantly opposed to any memorial. However we did not encounter the expected degree of denial. At least all the people we met were well aware of the elephant in the room, but did not know how to deal with it.

The drive between Banja Luka and Prijedor framed our days. Every journey we passed through the vale of Prijedor, the mine of Omarska on the one side and on the other Mount Kozara, where the fiercest partisan fighting and largest military losses in the Second World War took place, a costly victory, and site of the largest war memorial in the former Yugoslavia.

On this our first visit spring green began to cover the trees in the forests. Plum blossom sprinkled over orchards. Rivers swelled and muddied after heavy rains and the melting of snow. New Orthodox churches, like brightly coloured dinky toys, and newly constructed mosques, like meccano models, perched in the landscape. The now destroyed old Ottoman-style mosques, delicate but solid structures, used to inhabit the countryside, nestling among the undulating hills and meadows as though they had grown there.

Our project presented a challenge in that we intended to mediate between all communities equally. Bosniaks, mostly returnees, were a nuisance to the international community because they constantly made demands and threatened to destabilize the political status quo which protected and favoured former criminals and politicians who had conducted the war. This war had no clear victors or losers. Whereas after the Second World War, unconditional surrender, trial and punishment of the country's leaders, meant Germany could make a fresh start, Bosnia experienced delay and reluctance in bringing justice. The Hague Tribunal did its best to address this issue, but made slow progress in tracking down war criminals. Though some perpetrators of atrocities had been tried and convicted, many were still at large, including the chief war lords Radovan Karadjic and General Ratko Mladic, both protected by politicians who had themselves been involved in directing the war and sanctioning atrocities.

Our presence as mediators threatened the mutually back-scratching relations between Serb leaders and the international community. The British Embassy's representative in Banja Luka and the OSCE, Organization for Security and Cooperation in Europe's head of office in Prijedor greeted us with misgivings. Both told us our best ally would be the mayor of Prijedor. This advice almost cost us the life of our project. The mayor was alleged to be a war profiteer with close links to the Prijedor Crisis Staff which had organized the ethnic cleansing throughout the region. As Head of Post and Communication he controlled flow of information, and cut off contact with the outside world during the period of ethnic cleansing. So, far from being an ally, the mayor vigorously opposed our project.

However, by good fortune, substantial support came from the Office of the High Representative itself. Graham Day, the Deputy High Representative and Head of office in Banja Luka, enjoyed even better access to the criminals and political leaders than the ambassadors and OSCE. During the war he had been part of the negotiating team between the Serbs in Pale and the Bosniaks in Sarajevo, and had several times been forced to look down the barrel of guns held by drunken trigger-happy Serb soldiers, memories that sharpened his determination to bring criminals and still-free warlords to justice. He had no illusions about the corruption of present Republika Srpska politics, and the self-interest of the international community, and he bided his time, keeping his quarries on a long string. He valued our grass-root mediation knowing that progress could only be made by rocking the boat. 'Nervous Nellies', in Graham's words, preferred not to

upset the Serbs, whatever rights or claims the Bosniaks might justi-
fiably have. Our project challenged this state of affairs. The process
of mediation might eventually help the course of justice in this
beleaguered part of Europe, and wounds be given a chance to heal.

We arrived in Bosnia on the day political leaders of the
Republika Srpska threw out proposed police reforms which would
have united the police forces of both entities, Bosnian and Serb.
Paddy Ashdown, the then High Representative called it a 'black
day for Bosnia', but given the involvement of the police in atrocities during the war, it struck us as being an impossible hurdle to
clear until both entities faced up to the crimes committed and
justice had been at least seen to be done. The war continued in all
but name. As we approached Prijedor on our first day, we passed
busloads of already inebriated, red faced demonstrators, shouting
and gesticulating. Ringleaders from the flourishing Serb nationalist parties ferried them to Banja Luka to protest against the police
reforms. Since unemployment figures stood unofficially at around
60%, meaning that in reality they were even higher, plenty of idle
and discontented men could be found to attend such demonstra-
tions. Glad of a boisterous day out, fuelled with booze, they filled
the coaches, each preceded by a police escort.

We passed the small Bosniak town of Kozarac, which had been
flattened in the war, but was now experiencing a vigorous
rebuilding program. Returnees brought cash back from abroad.
Lorries bearing tiles, bricks and cement roared constantly past new
shops, bars, and houses. Kozarac bristled with defiance and
energy.

Two large new minarets fingered the sky, and an Orthodox
church, in baroque style, stood forlornly in the shadow of a larger
new one. Bosniaks had helped raise money to repair the old style
church, so Milorad Dodik, leader of the Alliance of Independent
Social Democrats (SNSD), ordered the building of the new one,
funded by Orthodox only. Then the Serbs claimed lack of funds
prevented removal of the other. More likely they felt uneasy about
destroying one of their own churches, so the striking proximity of
both buildings became a symbol of meanness of spirit, and ingrat-

itude at the attempt of one community to help reconciliation with its oppressors.

We entered Prijedor passing the mock medieval Hotel Sherwood, owned in its time by indicted criminals. Several tigers, a bear and a wolf in cages entertained guests at the casino. The hotel, known to be a staging post for drugs and arms, stood next to a gas-station, Egzotik, similar to dozens lining the road from the Croatian border to Banja Luka: gangster run and neon-lit in strident colours.

Shortly afterwards we passed Keraterm on the right, a tile factory where Bosniak and Croat prisoners had been held, tortured and killed in the war. A small plaque to the victims had been placed on a patch of grass outside the door. Keraterm, a long red-brick building, stood idle on the outskirts of town surrounded by grime covered factories and warehouses. The town could not disguise its decrepitude. Even the mine administration headquarters needed repairs, cracked steps leading to a rusty entrance. A crooked barrier half raised, stuck and broken, pointed rigidly at an angle over the entry to the car park. The pot-holed roads and grime turned Prijedor into a depressed third-world township. Young people slouched in cafes, watching and waiting.

DREAMS AND PRAYERS
A few nights before leaving for Bosnia I dreamt we were drinking tea looking out over a stormy sea, the waves steel-grey flecked with white-horse foam. Suddenly their agitation coalesced into a large wave like a black wall, rearing up to engulf us.

The first night in Bosnia I dreamed of an uncultivated garden turned into an overgrown meadow lying beyond another garden which had become water-logged. Nothing could grow properly, everything soaked and blossoms in the bud dropping off drooping branches.

Along with the support of the international community, which turned out to be a poisoned chalice, we felt the need of blessing from the religious leaders.

The mufti of Banja Luka could not be contacted, but two imams in Prijedor were prepared to meet us. We sat in their cramped office, the living room of a small house, and listened to a mournful litany of past destruction and murders and present discrimination from the Serb administered council. Funds had been raised from Sarajevo to rebuild a few mosques, but Bosniaks still found it hard to reclaim homes and property, on top of which there was no work for them, and priority would always be given to Serbs. They were not interested in our work

Bishop Jefrem, the Orthodox bishop of Banja Luka, was well disposed to us but showed no interest in our project and his denial of Bosniak suffering in the war shocked Emir Muhic, our Bosniak interpreter from Banja Luka. Aged twenty three Emir studied at Banja Luka University. No one could teach him any more there, but lack of funds trapped him in Banja Luka and he could not leave to study elsewhere. During the war his mother had returned from Croatia with ten year old Emir to care for her elderly parents who could not flee. Serbs beat the grandfather to death on the street outside their home and the grandmother died shortly afterwards from grief. A significant part of the project, Emir was not only a good translator but managed to convey the nuances of each speaker, and varied the tone of his voice, going pointedly high and shrill when lies were being told. He blinked, gasped and stumbled in translation when the bishop announced that 'the Muslims had imagined everything'.

Graham Day had warned us earlier of a rise in nationalism in Bosnia, particularly among young unemployed and the diaspora. This nationalism had now reached the same level as in 1992, the start of the Bosnia War. Metropolitan Nikolai of Sarajevo had used a commemoration ceremony at the Second World War concentration camp of Jasenovac to deliver a speech attacking the recently deceased Pope and to encourage old animosities. (Some Serbs claim that up to seven hundred thousand Serbs were killed at Jasenovac. But the Belgrade Museum of the Holocaust has a list of some eighty thousand dead, around fifty two thousand Serbs, sixteen thousands Jews, twelve thousand Croats and Bosniaks and ten thousand gypsies). Renaissance of nationalist fervour explained the presence of Bishop Vasilje at Zitomislice, busying himself distributing consecrated bread to the Serb politicians and shooting furious glances in the direction of the Federation police force protecting them. The religious communities in Bosnia were a repository of distilled hatred between the ethnic groups. They were not likely to support our project of mediation and reconciliation.

However, Bishop Komarica of the Catholic Church in Banja Luka, a significant exception, did bless us, as we knew he would. This gentle and untypical Bosnian Church leader had become the closest friend of the Soul of Europe in Bosnia from our first meeting six years earlier. The story of his resistance activities in the war had made him famous throughout Europe. His struggles with the Serb authorities as he tried to save lives, on all sides, are well documented. But the experience traumatized him. Despite his energetic, incessant activity, driving to all ends of his large diocese and also travelling frequently abroad on lecture and conference tours, the horrors he endured in the war and threats to his life had worn his spirits down. Now he perpetually recited the same mantras about the suffering of his community and everyone he spoke to had long since closed their ears to him. We always listened, with humility, remembering how this brave but modest man had regularly been seized by the Serb military, and while they prepared to shoot him he had gone from soldier to soldier, disarming each one calmly, laying the guns on the ground, saying a prayer and walking away.

He warned us of the impossibility of our task, and although he did not want to involve his priests in the project, knowing how it would stir up painful memories, he readily took us into his private chapel where under charred crucifixes, retrieved from burnt Catholic churches, and photographs of murdered priests and nuns, he prayed fervently for the success of our mission, ending with the Lord's Prayer: 'Forgive us our sins as we forgive those who sin against us.'

The bishop warned us about stirring up emotions, hurting people's feelings. 'Be careful how you go about this,' he said. We needed to be sensitive. A quarrel with either side could happen, and we must avoid trouble with anyone. The Serbs tended to hide, playing down their part in the war while the Bosniaks did the opposite. Croats, now the smallest minority in the region, had not even been asked what they thought.

ED VULLIAMY AND KOZARAC

Ed Vulliamy, the Guardian journalist, reported on the war in Bosnia and discovered Omarska the killing camp. He spent time in the company of Bosniak refugees fleeing across the mountains, ducking bullets and experiencing the ferocity of the ethnic cleansing from the victim's perspective. Because he had testified against several criminals in The Hague it was now dangerous for him to be seen in Prijedor. We met him in London on our way to Bosnia. Lean as a whippet, frazzled and intense he enthusiastically supported us; but although his opinion mattered, if Kemal Pervanic had stopped us, we would not have taken the project on.

The Guardian still printed occasional Bosnia reports from Ed Vulliamy, usually concerning the capture of major criminals with glamorously bloody pasts that made good copy, but showed no interest in our mediation project. Ed's partisan approach to coverage of the war led to Serb complaints that his reports were too sympathetic to Bosniaks and these may have influenced editorial decisions not to let him cover our story.

Ed Vulliamy regretted not being able to come with us; eager to revisit friends there. It had been the most intense experience of his life. His reporting of Omarska had saved an incalculable number of lives, so his bonds with the Bosniak community in Bosnia were insoluble. He suffered from frustration at the decline of interest in the western media for the continuing desperate conditions in Bosnia, shaking his head violently, wispy hair tousled, tears of distress in his eyes. He gave us names of significant Bosniak contacts. Since the international community could only steer us in the direction of Serbs, and showed little interest in Bosniaks, these names became our only lead.

Emsuda Mujagic, top of the list, directed Hearts for Peace, a

non-governmental organization based in Kozarac, funded interna-
tionally and run by women, most of them survivors of rape and the
killing camps at Omarska, Trnopolje and Keraterm. Every year in
May they organized a conference, gathering other local organizations together with friends and supporters from abroad. The event
included a visit to Omarska on May 24th, the anniversary of the
killing camp's opening, laying flowers, remembering the dead and
telling their stories.

Through Emsuda we made our chief contacts with those from
the Bosniak community who would become crucial to the success
of both the mediation process and the project to create a memorial
at Omarska

On our arrival the Hearts for Peace house in Kozarac heaved
with people, including several women members from the Hearts
for Peace branch in the United Kingdom. These women had coinci-
dentally invited us some months earlier to speak about our
projects in Bosnia at their conference centre Hazelwood House in
Devon. There they had played us a video of the first conference in
Kozarac, the town then still in ruins. The film showed rape victims,
young women, still traumatized, but some of them hesitantly
singing and dancing at a party on the last day of the conference,
trying to get the shame-faced Serb police who had been sent to
monitor the event to join in. The intrepid women of Hazelwood
House ran projects in all parts of the world, including looking after
Ukrainian children suffering from the fall-out of the Chernobyl
disaster, and communities in Palestine who lost their homes in
Israeli attacks. The women had been visiting Bosnia since 1993,
supporting rape victims and establishing contact with Emsuda
Mujagic, helping her found the Hearts for Peace centre in Kozarac.

After supper a choir of women in blue and red gowns lined
with black sang in octave unison, folksongs about love, a girl being
bitten by a snake while picking apples, a girl and boy arguing over
water, the girl saying: 'I hope you die of thirst because you cheated
on me.' The women beamed as they sang and most of the audience
joined in.

Emsuda Mujagic, a demure and quietly spoken woman looked

grim as we shook hands, but on realizing who we were burst into a smile, radiant and hopeful.

'We can help you with this hot potato,' she told us. 'The criminals are in charge, that's the problem.' She meant these to include the mayor of Prijedor and Serb non-governmental organizations, staffed by those involved in the ethnic cleansing and now continuing to be funded and protected by the government.

'The mentality of the torturers has not changed,' she went on. 'Good Serbs exist, but they are afraid, and keep quiet. Don't be manipulated, and don't give up! You deal with Serbs by being unwavering. Say to them that this is going to happen, and they must adjust to what you decide. Only then will you be accepted and taken seriously. The mayor should have been here. His crimes will be uncovered one day. He bides his time, hoping Bosniaks will give up.'

About Kozarac itself she told us all the young men had died in the war, two hundred and fifty from two streets alone. 90% of wives lost husbands and children.

'Talk to them,' she said, 'they are not bitter. Pity rather the criminal monsters. And help us build the memorial!'

THE WALL OF SILENCE

'In Italy Italians have the Mafia. In Bosnia the Mafia have Bosnia,' Kasim, Kemal Pervanic's brother, told us with a bitter laugh when we visited him in Kevljane.

While rebuilding the family home he lived in a metal shed, protected by a hidden gun and a tethered German shepherd dog with a loud bark and sharp teeth. The long muddy and bumpy road across fields passing row on row of burnt out ruins told returning Bosniaks: 'You are not wanted here, go away.' Kasim designed the house with many windows, so approaching danger could be seen from every angle. Now they looked over groves of neglected orchards and a large garden which the busy man on his own had no time to cultivate, across fields, some ploughed, to a mosque, distant hills and woods. In 1992 Kasim and others had hidden for a while in those woods, hoping to evade the approaching Serb army. Swifts nested in the house, darting in and out through the window gaps.

Kasim expressed pessimism about the future. Serb attitudes had not changed. Criminals were still at large, known by all, recognized on the streets by their former victims, who even if they complained and reported to the Serb authorities would be ignored by them.

Bosniak and Serb communities continued to live cheek by jowl, the Bosniak township of Kozarac close to the mainly Serb controlled Prijedor, and the Bosniak village of Kevljane, rising from the ashes, next to Serb Omarska, which had provided guards for the killing camp and now made up majority representation on the municipal council for the whole region. Twelve years after the war ended the stark fact remained that the two communities barely talked to each other, and then only about business, avoiding mention of what happened in the war, living together in two separate worlds. From Kasim's belligerence we could gauge Bosniak anger at the ethnic cleansing, and Serbs were right to be fearful about the future. The history of the region chronicled a perpetual cycle of revenge and counter-revenge. 'If you want a fight,' Kasim told his Serb neighbours, 'I will be ready for you!' Everyone was armed, and even peaceable Kemal told us he would not consider returning to live in Kevlanje without a gun. The head of the Organization for Security and Cooperation in Europe office in Prijedor, Jeff Ford, reported that local Bosniak mothers were bringing up their children to hate Serbs and exact revenge in the future.

A wall of silence now stood between the two communities. Croats represented such a small minority, their voices did not count, and most remained in Croatia where those who survived the killing fled, and the government there gave incentives to stay: houses and work. Bosniaks had no other home than Bosnia. In the war they fled to European countries which generally treated them with suspicion as aliens. After 9:11 Bosniaks became even more disliked and feared in Europe, all of them seen as potential terrorists. Many returned home to Bosnia, determined to renew their roots, and not to be driven out of their country again. Those that stayed abroad sent money to relatives and returnees, meanwhile nursing dreams of retribution. For them and those living in the Federation, Prijedor and the region could disappear down a black hole.

Our first meeting with Serb officials in Prijedor was with the chief of police. The police station had been headquarters for the policy of ethnic cleansing. Bishop Komarica told us how often he challenged officials there, pleading in vain for the lives of Croats and Bosniaks. Persecution, destruction and killing had been coordinated from here. These exclusively Serb headquarters had been established by Serb nationalists in advance of the war with the purpose of replacing the official police authorities in Prijedor. The elected Bosniak and Croat leaders were subsequently taken to Omarska, many of them murdered. After the war the illegal police station continued to function, because the international community did not reinstate the pre-war authorities, who had either been killed or fled.

The chief of police, looking steadily and suspiciously at us, remained hunched behind his desk while we sat with a couple of his officers, so we had to look sideways and over our shoulders when he spoke. The Republika Srspka flag hung ostentatiously on the wall, announcing that the region did not recognize being part of Bosnia.

We talked with the officers about our project and mentioned the white house.

'I don't know what this white house is. What are you talking about?' the chief of police suddenly interrupted, shrugging his shoulders, then immediately compounded his lie by telling us the house stood at least three miles outside the mine. 'We maintain law and order, and follow European laws in executing our policy,' he droned, yawning with impatience. 'Since the war we just follow orders, gather information, excavate bodies when we are told where they are. We are not authorized to answer questions.'

Eyes glazing with boredom, he then launched into a 'symphony of love' speech in which he described Prijedor as a place where

Bosniaks and Serbs lived harmoniously together.

'We are happy to talk with them. We protect all citizens and care for everyone's property. There are no problems between the communities. The situation improves daily between Serbs and non-Serbs. There are excellent relations between all ethnic groups. The police are totally impartial; cooperation is good with Bosniaks and Croats.'

To our comments about the war and its aftermath he demanded evidence. 'It was a civil war, and there is no record of inter-ethnic conflict. It was kept under control, and as for Omarska, visits were well supervised.' He did not say whether the supervision was to protect the victims or to encourage the perpetrators. Then he announced that Bosniaks and Croats even took charge of police matters. How did he know? 'We see it! It's getting better day by day. We have cooperation between all groups, and there are no serious incidents any more.'

Fed up with this recitation that he knew we all knew to be lies, he left us suddenly, having been called to another meeting elsewhere.

The remaining officers continued the re-writing of history by telling us how the mayor, Marko Pavic, had saved lives, and that 90% of the workforce in his businesses were Bosniak.

Concerning the police reforms they pretended to have no authority, describing themselves as a small unit without influence. 'Police are not allowed political affiliations'. Entry into Europe depended on the police forces of both entities combining but clearly the notion of sharing tasks with Bosniaks whom they had tried to ethnically cleanse could not yet be tolerated. Instead they complained about the heavy mass of documents landing on their desks from the Office of the High Representative, all needing to be read and signed: 'We are not paid to answer these kinds of questions.' But they wanted to join Europe anyway.

This police station did not look like a place where people spent any time at all reading documents. Nor did it seem that these former soldiers from Western Slavonia, Serbs driven out of Croatia, would have any interest in cooperating let alone uniting with the Bosniak Croat Federation, whatever the rewards of being part of Europe. They watched us steadily with a slight glint of mockery, reading our thoughts which could not help focus on whether these inscrutable men had themselves tortured and killed people.

We left the police station and returned to Kozarac where survivors waited to take us on a tour of the concentration camps at Omarska and Trnopolje.

LAYING FLOWERS AT OMARSKA AND TRNOPOLJE

A piercing scream tore through the quiet air. 'Where are you my husband, my son? What have you done to them?'

A solemn procession of survivors and visitors filed out of the bus and crossed a ditch into the field behind the mine where stood the white house. An overcast sky deepened the sombre mood. On our first visit with the mine manager we had seen the shed from inside the mine. It stood apart in a field, isolated from the rest of the work buildings. We now saw it from a different perspective, framed and backed by the looming mine offices and hangars, a part of the whole complex.

The woman screaming and wailing had to be comforted and held up by Emsuda Mujagic and Nusreta Sivac, a former judge who had herself been raped and tortured at Omarska.

Several women who were survivors pointed out other buildings in the mine where they had been systematically raped. They returned to take part in this visit every May from Germany where they had fled after the closure of the camps and now worked as nurses or cleaners in hospitals and schools. Dressed smartly and hair styled as for a special occasion, they marched between the mine buildings, defying guards and workers to stop them, searching out and identifying places where they had been held and others were also tortured, a number of them killed. Afterwards they told their stories.

Several women from Hazelwood House discreetly and respectfully accompanied the survivors as they laid flowers at the door of the white house. They had supported the women survivors since before the end of the war, crossing the border from Croatia regardless of warnings from UN troops about mines and being shot. On a visit to Sarajevo, while it was still being shelled by Serb militia from the surrounding hills, they helped bring medicines and clothing to the besieged city. Anabel Farnell-Watson remembered covering her luminously white hair so they would not be fired at during moonlit night forays on their way to a tunnel under the airport runway. This tunnel allowed transport of provisions from the countryside to the city centre and people could also escape in the opposite direction.

The Hazelwood House women kept faith with Emsuda Mujagic and the survivors who for years had tried to get local officials, who acted as caretakers of the mine before it was sold to its present owners, to allow them access to the white house and other places where family members and friends died, and where they themselves had suffered so much. The mine then remained resolutely closed to them, officials denying that anything had happened there, until the previous year when under the new ownership a group of survivors accompanied by international non governmental organizations were allowed to visit and lay flowers. The survivors now wanted a memorial, and welcomed our presence which promised a granting of their wish.

The Hazelwood House women were familiar with dangerous situations, but their shocked expressions proved how impossible it is to get accustomed to horrors. Gillian Keane had earlier approached the tiger cage at the Hotel Sherwood in order to photograph the mangy creatures for evidence of maltreatment so they could be liberated. She was forced to beat a retreat, though not before taking the necessary pictures, when she suddenly noticed the cage door had been left open and the keeper nowhere to be seen, leaving the hungry beasts to attack her. Outside the white house however she looked suddenly defeated, staring silently and accusingly at the mine officials and at the Serb police who supervised the visit, ensuring the Bosniak survivors did not roam around the mine, disturbing the workers and creating incidents.

Other visitors from abroad, including a young film crew, joined the procession. Most looked numb and sad; some carried on conversations, as though unable to deal with the pain being so audibly and visibly felt by the survivors. However a young woman in charge of the Agency for Democratization, one of the few non governmental organizations still active in Prijedor, turned her lips down and muttered the word Jasenovac, implying that what happened in Omarska (several hundred killed) could not begin to compare in scale and horror with the killing of seven hundred thousand Serbs in the Second World War concentration camp, less than thirty miles to the north. Playing the traditional numbers game in Bosnia was a way of cauterizing trauma. Arguing about whether more or fewer were killed avoided having to face individual suffering where even one person's torture or death is no less significant than that of a million.

The procession entered the mine canteen, a large building used for holding hundreds of mostly Bosniak prisoners; interrogation and torture taking place in the upstairs offices. The workers had just finished lunch and two women kitchen staff continued to bang pots and pans, crashing plates and cutlery throughout the flower-laying ceremony. Nusreta Sivac spoke for the survivors about what happened there, trying to make herself heard above the clatter.

Outside, after the ceremony of flower-laying in the canteen, the same woman who had wailed so piercingly at the beginning of the visit let out another shriek, pointing at the workers peering out of windows in another building across the yard and calling to them: 'Tell me where my husband is!' A Serb woman herself she had married a Bosniak and was therefore considered a traitor and enemy of the Serb people. Now Emsuda Mujagic and Nusreta Sivac looked after her in Kozarac. We tried to comfort her, and she smiled gratefully through her tears, especially when Donald presented her with an Anglican cross hung round his neck, thinking to bring some cheer. She put the cross in her handbag, snapped it shut and said: 'I'd have preferred an Orthodox one!'

The clouds lifted as we left Omarska and a hot May sun shone on the procession as it arrived at the neighbouring village of

Trnopolje, site of another concentration camp, an old school where women, children and elderly people were ostensibly held for future transport out of Bosnia, but was in fact a place where the women and girls were regularly raped.

The building still stood, though a ruin. Weeds and even trees grew inside. The window spaces stared vacantly. All around lay a meadow. Emsuda stood in the long grass and described being held there with her two children; how girls, as young as twelve, would be called to an office on the other side of the road where passing soldiers and local police could rape them. A mother had tried to stop her daughter being abused and was shot dead. People were killed here too.

Trnopolje had been a mainly Bosniak village, and now only Serbs lived there. The old school remained untouched since the war, no explanation or sign of what had happened there. The Prijedor municipality had recently erected a war memorial to Serb soldiers who died in the war, within a few yards of the building. Ambassadors and other invited members of the international community attended the unveiling of the monument, two stone eagles above a list of names, honouring Serb patriots. No one paid attention to the old school behind it, though knowing well what had happened there. Like the white house in Omarska, and the old tile factory at Keraterm, this place was ignored.

After the closure of the three concentration camps in 1992, the international community turned its back on them. Despite constant clamour and demands from victims and survivors no one else could be interested, leaving these places to crumble and be forgotten.

Opposite the school stood a new house, luxuriously furnished surrounded by a neatly cultivated garden. It belonged to a local Serb businessman. It seemed some people were making money in the region. Next to the old school the local authorities had built a new one, attended by local Serb children. Everyday attending classes they walked past the ruin with weeds growing through the empty window frames.

ANEL ALISIC

Now we began to receive a clearer picture. On the one hand denial by the Serbs that anything untoward happened: it had been war and people died on all sides. On the other hand harrowing stories of blood on walls, ripped clothes, people being dragged around by ropes tied to nails in their tongues and death by lottery.

Depressed, we kicked dust along the cracked pavements of Prijedor and considered the urgency of breaking through the wall of silence between Serbs and Bosniaks, looking for a key to open up the process.

We were following Anel Alisic, tall and lean, always stylishly dressed in a dark suit and white shirt hanging fashionably loose over his trousers. He walked ahead of us, his characteristic loping yet upright gait expressing both sorrow and defiance. This was his town. He had been forced to leave with parents and brother when the war started and became a refugee in America. Determined to return to Prijedor and burning with a sense of injustice, he finished studies at a Brotherhood of Zion Catholic school in Michigan and as soon as possible caught a flight back to Bosnia. He moved into the family flat in the town centre. It had been trashed by the former Serb squatters, but at least it was home. No one would ever shift him again.

Together with his doctor aunt and politician uncle, two prominent Bosniaks in Prijedor, he ran an organization called Familia which attended to the social rights and health of returnees. The Alisic family had been a powerful clan in Prijedor before the war, and even after the ethnic cleansing, by returning immediately the war ended, remained a focus of influence and support among survivors.

Serendipity plays a significant part in the mediation process and meeting Anel Alisic turned out to be the key to breaking down the wall of silence.

Relationships are a two way process, and although we depended on Anel for information and contacts, he needed to be sure about our motives. He had observed too many international agencies using Bosnia for their own purposes: money, adventure, and promises leading to nothing. The country was littered with unfinished projects. Our kind of project, threatened by local politics, would always be risky. Trust had to provide the solid framework for the project.

Anel steadily observed our behaviour and reactions to the people we met. His expression rarely shifted from outrage and grim determination, dark wells of eyes filled with unshed tears in a pale face. When rare smiles came, like unexpected shooting stars, he became a boy, giggling mischievously and conspiratorially. Bosnia's future lay in the hands of this generation, men and women in their twenties and early thirties, from all ethnic groups, Serb, Croat, Bosniak and mixed, too young to have been initiated or have contributed to the conduct of the war, but had suffered the same traumas as their elders: being uprooted, losing homes, family members and friends. These youngsters missed out on childhood and adolescence by having to endure the ravages of a ruthlessly nasty conflict, and then grew up quickly in order to take on responsibilities for survival as well as the devastating aftermath of war. With few exceptions (among them notably Emsuda Mujagic, Nusreta Sivac and Anel's aunt and uncle) their elders had either been decimated in the war, implicated in what happened or were simply too traumatized to be of any use. Grizzled warlords survived, still running the country with support from the international community who had little appetite for bringing them to justice and not finding anyone else to deal with: 'The devils we know.' Profiting from corruption and black market rackets, drugs, arms and people trafficking as well as contraband cigarettes and oil (hence the plethora of funky gas-stations lining the main roads), they had no interest in changing the status quo. So a democratic future for Bosnia with integration into the rest of Europe lay with Anel Alisic and his generation.

Anel met us for the first time at Emsuda Mujagic's Hearts for Peace conference in Kozarac, and he eyed us initially with suspicion. Many local Bosniak organizations were present, and Anel knew each and all of them. 'Are there any good Serbs who would be prepared to join the process?' we asked. 'Yes, I know many, I will introduce you to them,' came his surprising reply. We had assumed from the wall of silence that no Serb would be prepared to even talk with Bosniaks. However a few young Serbs were ashamed of what happened during the war. The majority of young people tended to be even more fervently nationalist than their parents, some clamouring for secession from Bosnia and union with Serbia but this minority still in their teens, did not share these bigoted sentiments, preferring to create a new Bosnia where all ethnic communities could live peacefully together as had been the case before the war. They befriended Anel when he returned to Prijedor. We were now determined to make him our project manager.

Sitting in Emsuda Mujagic's office discussing a strategy for meeting people, Serbs, Bosniaks and Croats, anyone who might be interested in mediation, my attention focussed on a child's painting of a scowling boy crouched by a ruined wall, cheek resting on his clenched fist. Beyond the boy and wall stood a tree with a bird luminously white against a menacingly black sky. The picture spoke to me of the slaughter of men and boys in Kozarac and the overwhelming burden of grief and rage bearing down on the young survivors.

We followed Anel as he walked down another dusty street in Prijedor and by chance met his uncle, Muharem Murselovic, known to all as Mursel, a sprightly man in his early fifties, a deputy on the local and national assemblies. Despite the darkly melancholic gaze of a perpetually wounded man, he radiated confidence. He took us for lunch at Cordas, the only Bosniak restaurant in Prijedor and gave us his take on the present situation in Bosnia and advice for our project.

Muharem Murselovic had been imprisoned in the Omarska concentration camp for the whole time it was in operation, from May to August 1992. Since most of his Bosniak colleagues, all leaders of the community including judges, teachers, lawyers, businessmen and doctors, were murdered there he himself expected not to survive, but the camp closed in time for him to be bussed out to Croatia. He waited until the war ended before returning home as quickly as possible to establish effective political opposition to the Serb authorities now running his town and the whole of the Republika Srpska.

He told us that if Bosnia did not seize this last chance for reform, intended to reintegrate the police forces and armies of both entities that only ten years ago had been killing each other, the situation would deteriorate for Bosniaks in the Republika Srpska and they would be forced to leave. Returnees already felt tricked by the international community who had encouraged some twenty nine thousand to come back to the Republika Srpska, despite all their suffering ('like asking Jews to return to Germany in 1945'). Now they waited in vain for justice and employment. Even those who had built homes and worked on changes to the constitution which would honour their human rights now planned to leave. 'In fear their eyes are large.'

Three thousand three hundred people were still unaccounted for and missing out of twenty thousand removed from the Prijedor region alone. 'Serbs insist that only three thousand three hundred had been murdered whereas the rest left of their own accord, and they exaggerate the numbers of their own dead, though these were soldiers falling in battle and not innocent victims.' He warned us that Serbs would bring up the massacre of Serbs outside Sarajevo in a concentration camp now converted into a law court, an irony not lost on the Serbs. The crime had been punished, but Serbs were not permitted to place a plaque there. Serbs ignored the fact that for three years they had besieged the city, indiscriminately killing thousands: men, women and children and incidentally a number of Serbs who lived there. However, mention of concentration camps now triggered a response that they themselves had been victims. Complete denial may have softened to an acknowledgement that crimes had indeed taken place, but they would justify these by claiming equally awful crimes had been committed everywhere by all sides.

Muharem Murselovic agreed that the white house required a memorial, having been the focal point of the concentration camp. But he warned us that a memorial would also raise problems with the Serb workers at the mine.

Now the significant character of Marko Pavic, the mayor of Prijedor, began to loom in the conversation, and his massive dark shadow proceeded to cast itself over the whole project.

'The mayor will not be interested in this project,' Muharem Murselovic told us. 'He was the one most responsible for everything that happened, the ethnic cleansing. He believed in his mission. I went to school with him, we know each other well. He is a devious and cunning person. You need to know that. I'm telling you this so you make no mistakes. I want you to have success! He used to work in the secret police during the last years of communism. He has fingers everywhere, in business, in politics. Everywhere!'

How to find good Serbs? Muharem Muselovic could only shake his head. 'It's a bad idea to deny crimes. Admit to all of them! The problem now is that the mine needs to operate, but crimes took place there. The memorial therefore should be modest, not to inflame a worse situation. Bosniak workers were killed by their own colleagues along with many top civil servants, judges etc. including the Bosniak managers of the mine.'

Muharem Murselovic knew all these people personally.

'The memorial needs to be at the mine, not in front of the town hall in Prijedor,' he declared.

Had the present mine director also been involved? 'He did not direct the mine at that time, his involvement was low-key.' Muharem Murselovic told us to bear in mind that the new owners of the mine controlled 51% of the mine. Serb nationalists held the other 49%. They would take over the mine once the present owners had left. The president of the 49% was also minister for Serb war veterans and represented the board on both sides.

'Be careful where you tread, because you might step on a human bone,' Muharem Murselovic warned, telling us how at a conference held by the Council of Europe in Prijedor two men from a Bosniak organization handed guests leaflets about the exhumation of murdered Bosniaks whose bodies had been found in a well. Bosnian Serb police broke up the meeting and arrested the men. Their crime was 'stirring up religious and ethnic hatred.'

ZORAN DJUKIC AND THE ROUND TABLE

'Good Serbs are here, but you need to find them!' After hearing Muharem Murselovic's depressing analysis we doubted Anel could muster any for us but he surprised us by inviting a number of them to meet us at Cordas for supper the next evening.

Cordas became our base, and we even spoke of a 'round table' there where everyone and anyone from all sides interested in mediation and our project could meet, informally, just to sit together and discuss those painful issues about the war and killing which most people feared to mention and tried to forget. Cordas provided cheap but fine home-cooking, tureens of soup, either clear or thick, with mounds of thick sliced bread followed by platters of steaks prepared in traditional mid-continental style, floured and stuffed with cheese, or fried squids with spinach and chips, and large bowls of chopped salads. Bosniaks in Prijedor were not generally teetotal, so beer, wine and rakija, a potent local fruit brandy, washed the food down in generous quantities. The perspiring overworked waiters had to serve a constant stream of customers, mostly holiday-makers from the diaspora coming to visit relatives and bringing money from abroad. But for all the rush and clatter the waiters managed to beam at us and greet us warmly in heavily accented German, picked up from years of flight and survival. In summer we could sit outside overlooking the road, hailing new friends and acquaintances as they cycled or walked by, but in winter the cold drove everyone indoors to be choked by fug and cigarette smoke.

First we met Vedran, a gentle giant, bearded like an Orthodox priest, a philosophy student who spent most of the time reading and writing at home, his way of coping with poverty and the corrupt provincialism of Prijedor. His father, Mladen Grahovac, whom we were to meet later, had been a dissident Serb politician in the war and lived in constant danger of his life from nationalist Serbs who considered him a traitor. After the war Mladen Grahovac presented himself as an ideal clean-slate candidate for a new politics, but the international community decided to keep the war-time leaders on, regardless of their criminal activities. He could not find work and the family lived below the level of subsistence. When asked how they survived the young people shook their heads and explained that in a region of large extended families people helped each other out, potatoes and fruit from the country, sharing whatever they could find. Meanwhile the country's leaders lived luxurious lives on the proceeds of corruption and crime. The young people smiled indulgently at our naivety asking such a question.

Katerina Panic, a Serb journalist, petite but tough, joined 'the round table', together with her Croat boyfriend, a student who worked part-time in a market kiosk. She knew so much about local politics we called her our 'data base'. Whenever a name or place was mentioned her mind opened like a computer file and she gave us all the necessary information. These facts helped us especially when it came to dealing with Mayor Pavic and local Serb businessmen and politicians. Sasha Drakulic, from a mixed Bosniak and Serb family, accompanied Katerina and her boyfriend. He joined the group after some hesitancy, needing to be persuaded of our abilities and competence. Being articulate and passionately opinionated he became the round table's most vigorously critical member, questioning every decision, in particular resisting easy condemnation of Serbs. He worked for a local TV station, hosting discussions, so he too became an important source of information.

The 'round table' grew in the following months, people joining and leaving, but most of them enthusiastic about the project. Among the significantly active members were Tijana, a student of English from Banja Luka, Nino Jauz, a young politician from the main Serb nationalist party, Zoran a student and lecturer in economics who worked part time as an interpreter at the mine headquarters, and the only other Bosniak member of the group apart from Anel, Elvir, a student who had returned from a more prosperous life in Norway and now worked as a bar waiter.

Finally that evening Zoran Djukic arrived. Anel had been particularly keen for us to meet him. By the end of supper it became clear we had found our management team. Zoran from a mixed Croat and Serb family studied economics, played in the Prijedor football team, his black hair cropped in imitation of blonde Beckham. Vedran was pleasantly surprised to see him at the 'round table', knowing him only as a sporty type and local heartthrob. Since meeting Anel, Zoran had become serious about political issues. He scrutinised us intensely. Could we be trusted? He spoke loudly about the necessity of Serbs acknowledging what happened, resisting their criminal political masters and making restitution to the Bosniaks. The memorial at Omarska should not even be up for negotiation. It was a necessity. Sitting with his back to the road he did not see passers-by and customers at nearby tables staring at him in alarm. I kept glancing in their direction in case one of them produced a gun and shot him.

Anel laughed at my fears and with a shrug said nonchalantly about the onlookers: 'Well, they can join us if they like!'

Discussion and arguments continued over the table until darkness forced us to return to Banja Luka. An atmosphere of intense emotion dominated this first meeting of the 'round table', as these young people began to trust us and sense hope. The group met regularly after and became a catalyst for the process of mediation, with its inevitable disputes and mutual suspicions. The 'round table' created an opportunity to develop working relationships and friendships which were strong enough to withstand arguments and disagreements so able to sustain the project through the subsequent fraught process of mediation.

MARKO PAVIC: THE MAYOR OF PRIJEDOR

'You can't do anything without the mayor's permission.'

All Serbs we met told us that. Bosniaks reluctantly admitted that the mayor of Prijedor represented the main obstacle in their lives. He was the Godfather of Prijedor.

In Prijedor Mayor Marko Pavic wielded virtually autonomous power. The cabinet, all appointed by him, did what he told them. His shadow fell across the whole region. Everyone feared him. He controlled the lesser mayors in surrounding towns and had the local politicians in his pocket.

A nervous group of journalists and petitioners waited outside the mayor's office, meetings being delayed, as normal. The mayor decided whom he saw. Without our connections with the new mine ownership he certainly would not have given us the time of day. Even so it required persistence to fix a time. The mayor's secretaries stood on their dignity and treated all petitioners with contempt. Gaining access to this formidable person remained a challenge throughout the whole project. He ran Prijedor like a personal fiefdom and demanded the respect due to a president.

The fearless women of Hazelwood House were responsible for the delay this time. They had marched as a group into his office with Emsuda Mujagic and other survivors to challenge him on a number of issues including a memorial at Omarska. For example, every year during the Hearts For Peace conference in Kozarac, local Serb authorities turned off the town's water supply, so women had to carry buckets over large distances, just one of a number of unpleasant inconveniences to discourage visitors attending the event. The mayor refused to acknowledge any responsibility for these petty actions. His presentations to the international community, including ourselves, described good relations between the communities, contradicting everyone's experience. So the women from Hazelwood House spoke up for the powerless victims, unimpressed by his intimidating manner, looked at him unflinchingly and noted his expensive hand-made shoes. 'I was trying to find his soul,' Anabel Farnell-Watson told us afterwards.

At our delayed meeting with the mayor, exhausted and irritated by this attack of women, he was in no mood to talk about Bosniaks or memorials.

We waited for several minutes round a large oval table in a smart reception room decorated with unusually fine abstract paintings. The mayor had taste. Eventually the door to his private office opened. He emerged, a bear-like figure, and shook our hands politely his eyes glowering. This blend of good manners and pugnacity implied: 'I am a gentleman, but be warned: don't get in my way!'

His secretary, an unsmiling woman, sat opposite the mayor at the table and watched us coldly, pen poised over a notebook.

Deciding the mayor had been harangued enough by the Hazelwood House women, we took a conciliatory approach and after making our presentation (at the mention of Omarska he breathed in sharply, folding arms over his chest) and ended by asking politely for advice.

'Glad to see you,' he said, the surliness emphasising a deliberate note of irony. We were the last people he wanted to meet.

While he spoke we needed to remember that this man had helped direct the crisis staff set up by Serbs in Prijedor at the outbreak of war to carry out the ethnic cleansing of Bosniaks and Croats.

Hunched over the table, head lodged deep into broad shoulders, eyes lowered, the mayor proceeded to deliver his speech for foreigners: 'We are all citizens of the same town, undivided. All are welcome. We work together.' He continued for some time to extol the Arcadian harmony of multi-ethnic existence in Prijedor. Then he said accusingly: 'We are now only known for all the bad things in the world,' implying this notoriety was unjustifiably exaggerated. Having denied the actuality of ethnic cleansing he immediately contradicted himself by announcing proudly how Prijedor came first in the whole of Bosnia in the numbers of returnees being welcomed back to the region. If there had been no ethnic cleansing, who were these returnees? This paradox dogged the project: on the one hand Serbs told us nothing bad happened, then, in the same breath, complained that the Bosniaks had committed equally atrocious crimes against Serbs. Denial and defiant self justification went hand in hand. Before any mediation between both sides could happen, we needed to dismantle this inconsistency.

The mayor then extolled the economic prosperity of Prijedor, how it exported more than it imported, and major international firms invested there, referring specifically to the new owners of the mine. The company had rescued the region from total unemployment and the mayor now had to tread a fine line between pleasing a major investor and preserving his authority. Mayor Pavic had made sure the mine depended on his good will, which solved the problem of who was in control: the mayor. The new mine management could not afford to make demands if they wanted a compliant work force. Their objective was to get the mine working at full capacity, and make sure profits repaid investment and kept share-holders happy. Local politics were a necessary nuisance, and the mine manager knew the necessity of pleasing the mayor. The clash of business and political interests emerged as another major issue affecting the project. The Bosniak community reminding everyone of the stark facts of what happened at Omarska made sure this issue could not be ignored by either the mine or the mayor. For that reason the mayor resented our presence throughout the project.

It became evident at this first meeting that we presented him with a major challenge. His past came to haunt him, and at the same time his future depended on peace and prosperity at the mine. We were a threat but we were also an opportunity. He needed us. For all his bluster and contrariness, his contradictions and truculence, he had a refined instinct for survival and realized we needed to be kept on side. He may have been one of the most dangerous men we met in Bosnia, but he was also the one least likely to harm us. Throughout the project he took care to cooperate with us and even to look after us. Our friendship with the mayor caused ructions in the Bosniak community, those in the diaspora excoriating us for it, but the locals appreciated the leverage it gave us in the process of mediation between the communities.

Politics are a crucial aspect of lives and for people to shrug them off as oppressive or seemingly irrelevant to human daily concerns only encourages the tyranny of politicians. So people in Prijedor who did not want to be part of the project gave politics as their excuse: 'We don't want to have anything to do with it! It is too political!' This surrender of responsibility had permitted the war and ethnic cleansing, and now also kept Mayor Pavic in power. Behind this attitude lay generations of history, stories and mythologies that shape the psyche and culture of nations.

Mayor Pavic told us how he had spent the war as a foot soldier on the battlefield.

'We have to build the future together,' he told us, implying that Bosniak returnees should forget what happened and not keep looking for justice. 'Serbs should be part of the project,' he insisted. Once again he attempted to cloud the issue and confuse us by making a series of impossible suggestions.

Firstly there should be a memorial to murdered Serbs in Sarajevo, about fifty of them slaughtered by vengeful Bosniaks in the final days of the war when the Serb army was in retreat. The mayor seemed to deny the siege of the city where Serb soldiers bombarded Sarajevo from the surrounding hills and killed thousands of citizens. When we reminded the mayor of the fact that a number of Serbs there also fell in the line of fire, he smiled patronisingly and told us: 'Serbs do not kill each other.' We informed the mayor our remit from the new mine owners did not include a memorial in Sarajevo.

Secondly he told us that after Srebrenica no more memorials should be built anywhere in Bosnia. Prijedor bristled with memorials: massive black marble plinths exclusively dedicated to patriotic Serbs dominated the town parks. He told us Omarska did not need a memorial, reasoning that it would disrupt the working of the mine, and so jeopardise the investment the new owners had made in the region. If Bosniaks liked they could put a small plaque there. The only memorial he would tolerate would be a shared monument in the centre of Prijedor for all who died and suffered in the war. The government of the Republika Srpska in Banja Luka had just passed a motion forbidding any memorials to innocent victims of war, only to soldiers. Since dead soldiers in the Republika Srpska were mostly Serb, and victims mostly Bosniak and Croat, this decision nipped the Omarska memorial project in the bud.

We suggested establishing a foundation, supported by the new mine management, which would benefit Prijedor and become a living memorial. The mayor considered this, but with reservations.

He did not want any memorial to Bosniaks. Full stop.

He then gave us further impossible conditions meant to discourage and make the issue of mediation and memorials disappear. His secretary provided us with the names of local non governmental organizations. Only when we had them all on side with the project would he reconsider any proposals. These organizations being predominantly Serb were unlikely to support us, as he well knew, and we could in fact expect a hostile reception from all of them. These organizations had become a refuge for war criminals unable to find legitimate employment. Their former war bosses now running the country rewarded them for their loyalty by putting them in charge of these non-functioning organizations, financed by the local authorities. This financial security allowed them to continue their nationalist activities.

The mayor added to our pointless tasks by demanding we discuss the matter of memorials with religious leaders and secure their goodwill. He knew as we had already discovered that the religious leaders would have nothing to do with a process they considered too political.

If we succeeded in garnering support from these unlikely sources he told us he might allow us to address the council, though he conceded we could meet his cabinet.

The mayor felt pleased with the meeting, having made his position clear without dismissing us out of hand. He promised we could see him whenever we liked. He repeated pointedly that there was to be no 'memorial centre', except to those Serbs murdered by Bosniaks in Sarajevo. He then stood up, shook our hands with a triumphant smile, and left.

AZRA PASALIC

'The mayor has taken more power to himself, even from the Speaker of the Assembly. He behaves like a tyrant.' So spoke the Speaker of the local Assembly herself, Azra Pasalic, whom we met immediately after the mayor. A Bosnian rather than a Republika Srpska flag hung behind her desk in a light and welcoming room. An autumn landscape glowed across the reception table in the centre of which stood a large bowl of fresh fruit instead of the usual dusty dried flower arrangement.

According to post-war regulations in Bosnia, the speaker of each municipal assembly had to be from a different ethnic group to the mayor. Azra Pasalic, Anel's aunt, was a Bosniak doctor who had worked in Prijedor all her life.

When the war started she had been ordered to pack ready to be taken to Trnopolje, which the Serbs called a transit centre from where Bosniaks and Croats could leave for other parts of the world. The ethnic cleansing started as a series of transports into Croatia, the camps being collecting points. These places deteriorated rapidly into opportunities for violent score settling; the collection centres turned into concentration camps and people who had once been in positions of authority were now humiliated, punished and killed. Azra Pasalic being a prominent figure in Prijedor found herself under house arrest where 'all bad things happened' to her. She left in a convoy on which some two hundred and fifty people were killed and the women abused. The survivors were dumped on the border with Croatia and she spent the rest of the war in Zagreb.

After the end of the war she returned to Prijedor, along with her brother Muharem Murselovic. Being the only Bosniak doctor specializing in pediatrics she considered this to be her primary task because Bosniaks feared going to Serb doctors. Politics were part-time. As one of the earliest returnees she felt impelled to fight for the rights of those brave enough to return to a place from which they had been brutally expelled. She shared their traumatic experiences. Her father and stepmother had been murdered in her home. She established her surgery there and allowed other rooms to be used by Familia, the organization she set up with her nephew Anel to advise returnees on their rights.

The contrast between Azra Pasalic and the mayor expressed a marked difference of class and quality. Azra belonged to a traditionally well-educated middle class that had run Prijdor for generations. Her relaxed manner, simply but stylishly dressed, self-confident and open-hearted was in marked contrast to the mayor, an apparatchik turned businessman in an expensively tailored suit and hand-crafted shoes, who had taken advantage of the collapse of communism, the chaos of war and its aftermath to make a fortune: a defensive, suspicious and intimidating man.

However, the mayor held all the power in Prijedor, and Azra Pasalic was no more than a token figure in the Municipal Assembly, backed by a minority of just five Bosniaks out of thirty one members, despite a new law insisting that local authorities should adhere to a policy of proportional representation. She could press for reforms to improve the lives of returnees, but the mayor had the final decision as to how and where money could be spent. So he siphoned international aid into amenities for Serb areas, leaving Bosniak and Croat communities without roads, and kept control of their water and electricity supplies.

Azra Pasalic made a point of talking to her Serb colleagues in the Municipal Assembly, and found most of them prepared to be friendly, though unable to talk about what happened in the war.

'This is a difficult process, take things slowly,' she advised. For instance the mayor accepted her invitation to attend the recent funeral of a hundred and twenty Bosniaks whose bodies had been identified from a mass grave. 'It was not easy for him. Do not expect too much. Look for the truth. Everywhere. Even in Sarajevo. Punish only the criminals, do not universalise guilt. We have to cooperate and talk.' Things were changing, even in Prijedor. Recently at a Municipal Assembly meeting she had been attacked by a Serb politician who claimed she lied about the murder of her parents. The assembly supported her. 'He embarrassed himself!'

Azra Pasalic, Emsuda Mujagic and the former judge, Nusreta Sivac, formed the core group of Bosniak women who would help break the silence with the Serbs.

THE BELLS OF OMARSKA
The tall slender form of Bishop Jefrem in full Orthodox regalia, chest clanking with large crosses, led his priests across a dusty field to the newly constructed church in Omarska: a timeless picture; a scene played out for centuries across Eastern Europe, the

bishop blessing poor farmers and barefoot children scampering alongside the procession.

Omarska was a town without centre, just a long street lined with small dilapidated houses. Amidst the poverty a few new and spectacularly smart villas stood out, signs of affluence among a lucky few, but raising questions about where this wealth came from and why it had not spilled over into the rest of the drab community. We had called in on the local mayor and found him to be a maths teacher from the local school in the company of an elderly male secretary. Both dressed in threadbare suits, the secretary looked surly, and the mayor seemed frightened and depressed. We sat in a dingy shed-like building that served as the mayor's office. Neither man could understand why we should be interested in them. They were too tired or scared to talk with us, saying that power lay in Prijedor, and neither of them could explain what their jobs signified. When we asked if there was anything the mine, whose massive walls and cranes loomed over the village, could do for the community, they looked even more afraid and muttered something about septic tanks needing repairing and that the town's electrics, untouched for fifty years, had become a hazard. The secretary looked at us suspiciously, especially at the mention of a memorial to victims of the concentration camp. They insisted no one in the town had any involvement in the killing, though we knew prison guards came from Omarska. But they wanted better relations with the present owners of the mine. This comment at last gave us a lead and we offered to set up meetings between the mine-management and community leaders like themselves to discuss future mutual benefits. But they looked disinterested and we could only assume they were stooges, with no influence or say in what happened in their town.

Katerina Panic, the journalist member of the round table, had informed us that Omarska represented the mayor of Prijedor's power base, and made up the majority of the Municipal Assembly. Apart from a bustling café on the outskirts of the town, and the scattering of ostentatiously smart villas, there was no evidence of

Omarska's local influence benefiting the rest of the community. However the timid mayor showed some interest in the consecration of the new Orthodox church. The building would give Omarska its identity as a purely Serb community. Across the fields we could see the minaret of neighbouring Bosniak Kevljane's new mosque.

Under a cloudless June sky children and villagers watched with wide-eyed curiosity as the bishop shook hands with local dignitaries before entering to bless the building. Nothing so exciting had happened there in living memory. Bishop Jefrem looked surprised too see us, pleased we had taken the trouble. He had invited us to attend the consecration at our previous meeting when he shrugged his shoulders, hands in the air on being told of our project, saying: 'I think Bosniaks should stop being imaginary victims.' For that reason we thought it best to take Katerina Jovanovic as our interpreter to the consecration rather than Bosniak Emir Muhic (who was only too relieved not to have to attend).

Katerina Jovanovic, a Croat, was married to Dejan, a Serb, who had administered our civic forum project in Banja Luka. Money for this project ran out and he found a post with the Office of the High Representative in Banja Luka. His wife's attractive looks and manner softened all the people we met, and they would even ask how such an ordinary guy had managed to hook such a pretty woman. Dejan gladly left his wife to do the interpreting because he guessed the service would last for at least three hours and he preferred to take their large bouncy puppy for a walk in the countryside. A mile outside Omarska stood a small antique wooden Orthodox church, decorated with 19th century paintings of rosy-cheeked saints flying through the ether. Large evergreen trees surrounded the church and provided shade from the intense summer heat, so Dejan chose to wait for us there.

Dejan and Katerina Jovanovic represented the liberal intelligentsia among Serbs, and yet even they played the numbers game, casting doubt on exactly how many Bosniaks were massacred in Srebrenica: 'Not seven thousand, only two thousand were killed!' Dejan insisted. 'The international community is lying!' as though this striking discrepancy of figures somehow excused the violence against even the lesser number. If this was what they thought, then how much stronger would be the denial among more nationalistic sections of Serb society.

As a Croat woman married to a Serb the couple were discriminated against everywhere, despite their impressive qualifications. In Banja Luka her Croat background meant Katerina Jovanovic could not find employment. In Zagreb, where she had family, Serb Dejan would be in a similar position, the Croats hatred of Serbs so great that until recently neither country had allowed visas to the other. Equally, Katerina would not be welcome in Belgrade. Dejan's position in the Office of the High Representative as a political officer would come to an end once it closed down as predicted in the coming year and he would be unemployed again. Katerina continued amassing further qualifications as an accountant, and meanwhile earned what she could as an interpreter. They smiled through their hardships, avoiding having children and kept a ménage of birds, fish, small animals and a dog instead.

To escape the stresses of life Dejan, a dedicated biker, took his big machine for noisy rides, his slight physique bulked out in leather, scarlet kerchief round a slender neck, delicate features creased in a mischievous grin, an improbable 'hell's angel'.

Bishop Jefrem led the procession and a rapidly growing crowd of worshippers into the church. At the entrance a beaming Serb businessman, who had paid for the bells, bowed and kissed the bishop's hand. The bells decorated with wreaths and ribbons stood in the middle of the church. The highlight of the subsequent three hours consecration was the blessing of these bells. While the service continued, they were hoisted noisily into the belfry, chains clanking, ladders creaking under their weight, and with an alarming thud as one of them fell to the floor of the gallery, but fortunately not breaking through and crushing the people below.

Some years earlier, Bishop Jefrem had taken us on a journey through his diocese to show us the many new Orthodox churches being built. Like the one at Omarska they were empty shells.

Outside they looked complete, but inside they were bare, not even plaster on the concrete, let alone paintings and decorations which traditionally covered the interiors of Orthodox churches. Bishop Jefrem consecrated one church after the other, leaving future generations to complete the task. His chaplain gradually warmed to us, though the drive took him away from wife and children whom he hardly ever got to see. Among his many tasks, like serving coffee and spirits to guests, he also took care of the bishop's wardrobe. Once having driven the bishop over a hundred miles to Belgrade for a meeting with the patriarch, a vestment was missing and the bishop ordered him all the way back to fetch it. The priest appreciated our gratitude for the sacrifice of his domestic time and broke off branches of the acacia blooms that hung low over the road, handing them to us smiling broadly, eyes shining with friendship. The frothing fronds of snow-white blossom filled the car with a heady scent.

The fragrant blizzards of acacia hanging along the road to Omarska a month before had now faded, shrivelled by the June sun, and given way to chestnut blossom. This same chaplain now intoned the opening chant of the liturgy in a baritone of such intense stridency that the congregation immediately came to attention. The bishop insisted on a high quality of performance; the liturgy sung with robust conviction. Another priest, trained at the Bolshoi Opera in Moscow, continued the chant in sonorous deep bass tones. The Orthodox liturgy represented a unique aural tradition, the cultural heart of Bosnia, just as visually the round-breasted domes and delicately pointing minarets of Ottoman mosques that once nestled in the country's rolling hills and valleys celebrated an Islamic tradition of art in the same country.

Despite its wealth and influence, the Orthodox Church in the Republika Srpska felt ignored and patronised by the rest of the world, so our presence pleased all the priests who welcomed us with cheery waves and warm hugs. It turned out in private conversations with them that they missed friendly relations with Croats and Bosniaks, talking nostalgically of pre-war times when the religions coexisted peacefully. They were still happy to engage with everyone but the bishop forbade any dialogue or friendship. All religious leaders, Croat Catholic, Serb Orthodox and Bosniak Muslim, laid down the law and expected total obedience. Politics ran religion in Bosnia. Time and again the response to our proposals from priests and muftis was: 'We cannot do anything without permission...'

After the consecration the crowds dispersed out of the church leaving Mayor Marko Pavic to take photo calls with the bishop who insisted we join in. The mayor smiled, gratified by our presence. Our gesture of friendship to the Orthodox Church may have been a small one, but it carried sufficient significance with the Serbs for them to be at least well disposed to us. Meanwhile the maths teacher mayor of Omarska, whom we spotted hurrying past us in a crowd, nervously responded to our greeting. He would rather not have been addressed by us at all. His frightened glance in our direction said: 'Now you know who the power is here! I am a nothing.'

A gigantic banquet had been arranged outdoors under awnings, rows of tables and benches enough to seat several hundreds of guests. Pigs and lambs roasted on spits, and bands of sweating young waiters served everyone with limitless quantities of beer, wine and spirits.

'Who on earth is paying for all this?' cried Katerina Jovanovic.

Omarska had been invaded by the powerful and influential from all over the region, people who rarely if ever came to that otherwise neglected community. In all its history no one had paid the place so much attention, nor would this event ever happen again.

Bishop Jefrem took the seat of honour at the high table with Mayor Marko Pavic on his left. The mayor was muttering conspiratorially to a political colleague while they both tucked into chunks of meat and bread. Half way through the feast chefs solemnly carried two roasted piglets, spread-eagled on large slabs, to be blessed by the bishop.

We were seated further down the table along with the mine manager, who turned up after the service along with the mine director and others from the mine administration. The director was especially pleased to see us, rushing to shake our hands and embrace us like long lost friends. This marked a fundamental shift of attitude to us from our previous meetings.

The last time we met these staff members happened at a supper given by one of the new owner's chief executives. He had personally invited us to carry out the process of mediation. The supper was meant to bring the directors from the Serb run Omarska mine in the Republika Srpska together with the managers of the Bosniak run Zenica steelworks, in the Federation, under the same ownership. Immediately each group separated, the Serbs at one end of the table, the Bosniaks at the other. We and non-Bosnians sat wedged like a buffer in between both groups. The chief executive made a pointed speech about this division. 'Cooperation is all important! Next time I want to see you mixed up together,' he said, eyes flashing. 'We want this operation to succeed and keep our shareholders happy.' Looking at the hostile faces of the Omarska administrative management made us realize the impossibility of our task. The chief executive backed our project and pressure from above changed attitudes in the mine radically. The mine manager dressed down his staff in front of us, telling them they had to cooperate and give us all the help we wanted. By the time we met them again at Omarska they were all smiles and handshakes.

'You need to have the support of the mayor and all enemies of the project,' the mine manager told us. 'You have only begun to scratch the surface.'

At the Omarska feast he radiated optimism, informing us of a successful meeting with Mayor Marko Pavic. 'I am delighted with him!' he beamed. The mayor had agreed on all points. We were astounded at this sudden about turn only to hear that though the mayor did indeed support the idea of a memorial, it must be for all war victims, Serb as well as Bosniak, and that it should be in Prijedor town centre, not the mine, so production of iron ore would not be disrupted. The survivors of Omarska would not even remotely agree to any of these points, but the mine manager was pleased with the mayor: 'a rational and practical person!'

Among the guests seated at the tables we recognized a number of mine workers we had talked to, gauging their opinion about mediation and a memorial. All had denied killings at the white house, which they insisted had been a collecting centre from where Bosniaks were helped to go abroad and make lucrative careers for themselves. The workers deflected questions about tortures and missing bodies by insisting on a memorial for the Serbs slaughtered in Sarajevo. 'When you build a monument there, I will be the first to welcome a memorial here,' one said. Another proudly introduced himself as a 'soldier for Karadjic'. Recently on national television in Serbia and Bosnia footage of an atrocity had caused controversy. Filmed as a memento by a Serb soldier it showed his colleagues marching a file of young Bosniak men into a forest and shooting them in the back of the head. What most upset Serb viewers, who had up till now mostly denied such atrocities, were the verifiable identity of the soldiers, their voices, laughter and racist taunts, which proved the film's autheticity. The Serb media immediately turned up another piece of documentary film showing Bosniaks executing a Serb soldier, cutting his head off. The mine workers dismissed the first film as fake and expressed fury and distress at the other one. 'Are we expected to do nothing about this?' The general attitude remained that Germans in the Second World War committed more crimes than the Serbs, and therefore any criticism of Serbs amounted to a witch-hunt. They also quibbled over words insisting that ethnic cleansing and genocide were not the same. And what about all the crimes committed against Serbs?

The week before the Bosnia War broke out Kemal Pervanic had gone to have his teeth checked. His dentist Milomir Stakic became mayor of Prijedor and persecutor-in-chief of Bosniaks, sending Kemal, his brother and other Bosniaks and Croats in truckloads to Omarska, causing the death of hundreds. The Hague Tribunal punished Milomir Stakic with life imprisonment. For every criminal tried and sentenced there were dozens still walking free, some possibly at the banquet at Omarska.

Mayor Marko Pavic and the mine management could obstruct a memorial at Omarska but the matter of missing bodies kept the issue of justice and a memorial alive. Many survivors believed that bodies would be found in the mine itself. The chief executive dismissed this claim: 'We will not allow pressure groups to disrupt the working of the mine with rumours.' He reassured survivors by saying that if miners discovered remains they would be informed.

However several Bosniak agitators possessed lists of names of drivers at the mine who knew where bodies had been buried. We met one of these agitators, a soldier, Sabahuddin Garibovic, who had taken the Guardian journalist Ed Vulliamy to Omarska while it functioned as a concentration camp, so alerting the world to its existence. Sabahuddin lost his younger brother there. A memorial was all Sabahuddin wanted; a place to visit and remember, to lay flowers and maybe find closure. For that reason he persisted in trying to negotiate with the mine and not stir up bad feelings. 'Bosniaks used to be employed by the mine and should be allowed to work there again.' But if he got no satisfaction he would reveal the names of the drivers. Sabahuddin Garibovic, an experienced soldier with film-star looks, a Bosniak James Bond, had agreed to meet us in a café at Kozarac, just a few miles from Omarska. He kept us waiting then suddenly slipped next to us at our table, we did not know from where. He also left equally mysteriously, dematerializing. Not all Bosniaks behaved like victims. We began to meet many who were prepared to continue the fight, exact revenge and insist on their demands being met. The issue of a memorial at the mine would not go away.

Not one Bosniak had been invited to this party and Katerina Jovanovic our interpreter was probably the only Croat present. The consecration of an Orthodox church acknowledged the identity of one ethnic group only. To celebrate this event symbolically the chefs presented the bishop with a large cake baked in the shape of the church bells which at that precise moment began to ring out over the surrounding countryside. Everyone stopped talking and rose to their feet. History resounded at this moment. For centuries the pealing of bells by Serb Orthodox churches had been forbidden by the Ottoman rulers. To summon worshippers, priests used to strike large planks of wood together. The violent clacking echoed startlingly over hills and dales, less an invitation to prayer than a call to arms, a reminder of oppression and the need to resist and drive out the foreign occupation.

New church buildings were a visual statement of the Serb nation's presence and dominance, now bells proclaimed Serb triumphant repossession throughout the land.

The bells pealed as the party continued and people from Omarska gawped at the groaning tables and rows of outsiders, most of whom they had never seen before. Beyond the marquee a plentiful supply of beer and fruit brandy kept these locals occupied. Already some were reeling drunkenly, staggering towards the banquet with flushed faces and wildly waving arms. Menacing men in dark glasses forcibly restrained and pushed them away from the invited guests.

Mato Jasovic, the young priest of the new church at Omarska, looked bemused, an observer, sidelined like the town's mayor. Mayor Marko Pavic and Bishop Jefrem ran this show. Afterwards the crowds dispersed and caterers cleared the place so that it seemed no one had been there, and the town returned to neglect.

That evening Mato Jasovic visited the church and just as he was about to enter suffered a heart attack and died on the steps.

A STATE MEMORIAL AND A HOUSE OF BONES

Opposing worlds exist side by side in Bosnia. No more poignant example is situated a few miles East and a few miles West of Prijedor. The Bosniak township of Kozarac stands on the slopes of Mount Kozara, site of the bloodiest battles between partisans and fascists in the Second World War, and where the partisans endured a pyrrhic victory. Germany lost the war, but tens of thousands of Serbs, together with Jews, Bosniaks and those Croats who resisted fascism, died there. The road to Kozara runs through Kozarac passing mosques and Bosniak graveyards on its winding way though a thick wild forest to a gigantic monument on the summit of the mountain. This memorial became a symbol of unvanquished

Greater Serbia in the Bosnia War. Serbs effaced a number of the names of non-Serbs killed there and transformed one of the underground bunkers into a gallery filled with photographs and papers documenting the suffering of the Serb people at the hands of Germans, fascist Croats and perfidious Bosniaks.

The monument, a brooding grey concrete structure, towers over the surrounding forests and has at its centre a mysterious symbolic circle, accessible only to the very slim who are able to squeeze through ever narrowing corridors from the outside. Those who stand in the circle see no way out. However, once they step outside the circle the exits suddenly appear like slits in the concrete, and provide escape.

Parties of school children play football and picnic around the monument. All come from Serb schools as Bosniaks refuse to visit this shrine to Serb nationalism. Occasionally these children scamper down the steps to the bunker to look at grisly pictures of mutilated corpses, partisans with eyes gauged out, and grinning Mujaheddin standing next to piles of severed heads. Orthodox and nationalist flags decorate the walls and among the political propaganda a photo of Hitler sitting next to a mufti, clearly both happy to be meeting. The overall effect of this exhibition arouses feelings of anger and revenge, and a large visitor's book testifies to the success of this intention with page after page of exhortations to rise up and massacre all Bosniaks ('kill the Turks') and create a pure Serb nation. The Office of the High Representative knew about this exhibition when it opened, and officials attended the opening. It was judged not to be important, offensive or dangerous enough to close down. In England or any other western European country the organizers would have been punished. For as long as children are brought up with these searing images and inflammatory sentiments the cancer of ethnic hatreds will not heal and the threat of violence will persist in Bosnia. The present Kozara Memorial purposefully prepares for the next war.

A group of nationalists worked for that assiduously in Prijedor and agreed to meet us above the Metropolitan Café, another funky new bar where burly men in jeans and black leather jackets smoked and scowled while slender anxious girls in short skirts sat by the bar trying to attract clients. Upstairs the Serb and Republika Srpska flags hung on the wall next to pictures of St Lazar and photographs of Orthodox Church ceremonies, the link between religion and nationalism indissoluble. Told that we knew Patriarch Pavle personally, the group's leader felt emboldened to make a speech about the necessity of creating a racially purified Greater Serbia. Anel Alisic and Emir Muhic gritted their teeth, only too familiar with this kind of speech. Everyday Emir went to school the local butcher's son taunted him: 'Come over here Muslim boy and let me slit your throat!'

After the meeting the group's leader, realizing it had gone badly, phoned up the mine management demanding to know the names of all concerned with the project, and Anel began to receive threats and warnings which he shrugged off with characteristic nonchalance. Threats came from both sides. Young Serbs involved with us were told: 'You are marked!' Bosniaks wanting closure of the mine began to threaten the project, demanding that no Serbs should take part.

Kozara is under ten miles to the East of Prijedor; about twelve miles to the west of Prijedor is Sejkovac, across the border between the Republika Srpska and the Federation of Bosnia. Here in a warehouse eleven hundred bodies lay on the floor and stacked up against the walls. These had been disinterred from mass graves, victims of ethnic cleansing for a Greater Serbia.

The road ran next to the River Sana and as we passed the village of Alisici, Bosniak Anel announced: 'This is my aunt's home!' We turned the corner and passing through the next village Misha our Serb driver told us: 'And this is where my uncle came from!'

Flies buzzed around the open windows of the warehouse, skulls and bones lying on tables, a church-like silence pervading the vast spaces where sacks and shattered skeletons lay in rows, underwear, ragged remnants of clothes and a few belongings neatly placed by each one.

The shock of seeing the end result of the ethnic cleansing layed out so eloquently caused me to have a sobbing fit outside the warehouse. Anel came and put his arm round me. At that moment, observing my tears, he decided to be our project manager.

Aron Brzovic, a young journalist from Zagreb who insisted on coming with us, also broke down. He came from a Jewish family, one of a minority who survived the Second World War, thanks to the protection of Serb partisans. Emir took a dislike to Aron, considering him to be a frivolous adventurer, only interested in the thrill of seeing dead bodies and without commitment to the project. Aron did in fact disappear afterwards, deeply disturbed by what he saw. Through his tears he made several observations. 'These people should not be dead. They should be sitting in cafés drinking coffee, enjoying the sun, talking, living their lives.' And on the way back he spoke of the endemic cruelty of the Balkan male, his enjoyment in inflicting pain, the need to prove that 'he can do what he wants'. He remembered a calf needing slaughtering at home when he was a boy. The butcher spent some time in the shed, then when he had completed the task came out with a look of vicious triumph and bloodlust in his eyes that shocked the boy Aron. The look said: I am the master! 'There is something wrong with the Balkan male,' Aron sighed. 'Something sick...'

On the way back to Prijedor we overtook an elderly farmer striding down the road with a scythe over his shoulder. Behind him flowed the River Sana, glittering in the afternoon sun.

We passed a Serb Orthodox monastery and noted several large Republika Srpska flags fluttering over the chapel. They announced we had crossed the border from the Bosniak Federation into Serb Republika Srpska.

At this monastery some years earlier we met with the Orthodox bishop who would not support us because of our involvement with Muslims. However he insisted the Church had nothing to do with politics.

Back in Prijedor we met members of Izvor (Bosnian for 'source'), an organization devoted to finding bodies of missing people and informing their families. Izvor's most demanding task involved telling families that their missing relatives had been identified in Sejkovac. Seida Karabasic, a director of Izvor, spoke in a low monotone, face devoid of emotion that had long been drained from her after so many harrowing visits to grief-stricken survivors. Though finding out the grim truth was always hard, the worst trauma remained not knowing.

Seida Karabasic's words reminded us of the agonising screams of the Serb woman at Omarska, calling for her Bosniak husband and sons all murdered there, begging the guards at the mine to tell her where they had put the bodies so she could bury them.

TRUTH AND CONSEQUENCES: THE MASS FUNERAL

'Let's be clear about one thing: this was not a civil war but a war of ethnic cleansing,' we announced.

The members of Mayor Marko Pavic's cabinet sitting opposite us at the long conference table next to the mayor's private office drew a sharp collective intake of breath. No one had dared speak to them like this before. The visit to Sejkovac had steeled our resolve to cut through the denial and fudging of truth that kept the wounds of Bosnia festering.

The cabinet members stared at us in shock and disbelief at our gall as we ordered them to go to Sejkovac and stand among the bones, the material consequences of ethnic cleansing.

'It is a matter of humanity. This concerns the shared future of your community.'

The mayor, as a favour to us, had permitted us to meet his cabinet of mostly Serb nationalists, handpicked by himself, with one token Bosniak required by law of each Serb controlled municipality. Since this Bosniak, Mirsad Islamovic, kept quiet throughout the meeting we did not know which of the grim-faced people opposite he might be.

Afterwards he invited us to his office for a private chat because he could not speak freely in the company of so many Serb nationalists, and told us that the man sitting two seats down from him at the table had ordered his execution in Keraterm. Only the closure of the camp stopped that. Mirsad Islamovic's younger face looks out hollow-eyed from the crowd of prisoners behind the alarmingly emaciated Fikret Ali on the now familiar photograph that alerted the rest of the world to the existence of killing camps in Bosnia. Mirsad Islamovic lived in Sanski Most in the Federation because he still feared being harmed if he stayed in the Republika Srpska, preferring to commute twenty miles each day to work.

The rest of the mayor's cabinet responded furiously to our invitation to visit Sejkovac.

'What about the massacre of Serbs in Sarajevo?' the man who had ordered Mirsad Islamovic's death demanded of us.

Two women were present, one being Liljana Babic the vice-mayor, who chaired the meeting, nervously deputizing for the mayor. The other, Biljana Malbasic, who had been violently jabbing a notepad while we spoke, erupted in fury and accused us of upsetting them. 'You have stirred up bad emotions. Terrible things happened in the past to everyone, we have to forget and move on!'

'I did nothing wrong and refuse to take responsibility for other peoples' crimes,' she insisted at the end of a hysterical tirade.

The others, apart from Mirsad Islamovic, agreed with her, and several even denied anything bad happened at Omarska, and could give no explanation for the bodies at Sejkovac.

The memorial issue became the sticking point in our conversations with Serbs – and eventually Bosniaks too.

Considering the baleful influence of the massive black and grey marble plinths littering Prijedor's public spaces, let alone the Kozara Monument, people might have a point about placing a ban on any further memorials. But Serb insistence on one in Sarajevo to Serbs who had been killed there showed up the hypocrisy of their argument.

With the exception of Mirsad Islamovic, these members of the mayor's cabinet had fought for ethnic cleansing, as we reminded them at the beginning of the meeting, and therefore were likely to resist any reminders of an Islamic past in their country. They felt no regrets about ethnic cleansing. They were in a majority and ran the place now. The international community supported them. A memorial at Omarska would force an acknowledgement that they had done something wrong. So demands for a memorial there had to be resisted by them at all costs.

Our provocative confrontation with the mayor's cabinet had repercussions. It could have been a misjudgement, but we felt this to be the right time for straight talking. Due to the sensitivity of the issues we always referred to Anel and Zoran whose advice and candour we valued, though final decisions were made by us. They told us that no one dared talk so openly about crimes and ethnic cleansing. Mediators have sometimes to act as catalysts. This meant raising issues however provocatively. The trick is choosing the right moment. We could not be sure we had done that, nor whether our challenge damaged the process, or ourselves for that matter. The mayor, hearing about it, might realize we had to be taken seriously, since we were not afraid to speak our minds. He could also order us to be run off the road.

However a different set of threats to our work came from the Bosniaks. Mirsad Islamovic belonged to the SDA, the nationalist Bosniak party of Bosnia. We hoped he might reassure those members of his constituency who feared we were being too soft on Serbs that this was not the case. It turned out that divisions among the Bosniaks would cause most disruption to the mediation project. Those who did not live in Prijedor wanted the mine closed, even if it meant ruining the region's economy. Many wanted revenge. Bosniak mothers raised sons to prepare for the next war. Bosniaks were returning in large numbers to the region, eager to re-settle, start businesses and take control again. Their truculent determination, demand for justice and anger at the apathy, indifference and cynicism of the international community towards their situation, meant the possibility of war could not be ruled out.

'Do you really think Serbs would agree to a memorial?' Rezak Hukanovic, survivor of the white house, where he was beaten almost to death, and author of *The Tenth Circle of Hell*, looked doubtfully at us through a haze of cigarette smoke at Cordas. 'They might be prepared to accept a proposal, but then complications start and you will be hitting your head against a wall. The problem with this region is that war criminals are heroes in each others eyes; warmongers are still in power and not the peacemakers. The international community collude. We are not cut off from each other. Serbs come to Cordas, we go to Serb cafes. We can even have normal conversations, except when we retreat to our fortresses.'

Rezak Hukanovic had fled to Sweden after being released from Omarska. He wrote about his experiences and made a documentary film, *Killing the Light*, then left his wife and son there in safety to return home. Now he ran an independent television station, agitated against the war criminals still in power, and continued to live in Prijedor rather than the safety of Sanski Most, despite harassment and death threats. On one of our visits a bomb exploded outside his house. People were attacked occasionally but mostly harassment took the form of nasty phone calls or text messages and petty intimidation tactics, the purpose being to frighten returnees away and discourage others from coming back.

Large numbers of Bosniaks happened to be visiting Prijedor that June. They gathered on a football field at Kozarac for the funeral of forty nine relatives, murder victims, who had so far been identified at Sejkovac from over four hundred and fifty bodies discovered in the mass grave outside Kevljane. Two Catholic murder victims were also to be buried. Forty seven green coffins and two black ones lay in a long row in the middle of the field. Dignitaries from the international community stood in the relative shade of a few trees on one side with journalists, muftis, Bosniak politicians from the Federation and a few Catholic priests. Opposite stood a line of imams and a large crowd of mourners behind them. The sun beat down on their grief and fury. The speeches inflamed them further with talk of 'neither forgetting nor forgiving'.

Mayor Marko Pavic turned up with his secretary. He looked sheepish, hovering on the sidelines. But the Bosniaks appreciated his presence which meant that he acknowledged and no longer denied what happened.

After the ceremony a procession carried the coffins to their final resting places in villages across the region. We attended a burial in a meadow on the outskirts of Prijedor and watched the men's arms reaching up to the sky, hands outstretched, allowing the coffins to move in a delicate rippling motion along the hundreds of swiftly moving fingertips, like fields of wheat undulating in a breeze or sea anemones swaying in currents of water.

The women mourners stood drenched in tears, as the men leapt into the freshly dug graves and vigorously began to cover the coffins with earth. An intense silence accompanied the burial; no one spoke or wailed.

Afterwards we sat in Anel's flat overlooking Prijedor towards the range of hills around Mount Kozara. The view took in a century of violent history: Serb, Croat, Bosniak and Jewish partisans sacrificing themselves in thousands to stop the German advance in the Second World War; and the worst ethnic cleansing in Europe since that war, this time of Bosniaks and Croats. Anel and Emir sat thoughtfully, silently and sadly on the balcony as we rested. Distant calls of the muezzin drifted over the fields and rooftops from the neighbouring township of Kozarac.

BREAKING THE ICE

HISTORY AND TRUTH

July 2005. The next stage of the mediation process took place against the background of suicide terrorist bombs in London and Egypt.

The tender shoots of corn planted out in May now stood sturdy and tall, resisting unexpected hail-storms that had ruined other crops. Misha, our driver, complained of a dearth of plums in the orchards, which meant there would be no rakija that year.

He drove us along the familiar stretch of road from Gradishka on the Bosnia Croatia border to Banja Luka, meringue clouds banking on the horizon, pink-tinged indigo with flashes of lightning over distant mountains. Seven years ago there had just been small houses on either side, women gardening or feeding hens and men on hay carts drawn by horses. Now we counted nineteen garishly lit gas stations with names like 'Rolex', a plethora of coffee bars, new houses, a mosque rebuilt in Saudi style on the right, a Catholic church and convent being repaired on the left where nuns had been raped and the priest murdered in the war, and another Catholic church where nuns cared for drug addicts from all over Bosnia. Storks reared their young in a huge nest on a ruined pillar specially left for them in the middle of a large meadow.

Seven years ago the road from Banja Luka to Prijedor passed burnt out villages and neglected fields. Now Bosniak returnees were energetically rebuilding their communities, pigs snuffled and hens pecked in orchards and large tethered cows grazed in meadows strewn with wild flowers and herbs, masses of blue cornflowers, yarrow, hawkweed, tall mullein and fennel bordering the roadside.

At the Omarska turning a rich Serb entrepreneur was establishing a new township, Zeljograd, named after himself, with warehouses, cafes and a half-built hotel in Chinese style. Surrounded by dusty fields the place had the clap-board unreality of a Wild West film set. It stood only a few miles from the neighbouring Bosniak communities of Kevljane and Kozarac.

Our management team Anel and Zoran were in the process of setting up the first mediation meeting with the miners at Omarska. Members of the 'round table' agreed to be present, most of them young Serbs who were in favour of a memorial to Bosniaks killed at the mine.

History and myth mesh inextricably in Bosnia, which makes it hard but even more necessary to get at the truth. Nationalist perspectives, claiming that Bosnia had three different concurrent histories, favoured myth over facts. The person who tells the history interprets from his or her particular group. Who to believe? How to learn the truth?

The women from the mine management had swallowed Serb propaganda from before the war about the threat of a violent Bosniak takeover of the former Yugoslavia. Several were still consumed by bitterness and fear but three agreed to meet Emsuda Mujagic and Nusreta Sivac.

First we spoke with Mladen Grahovac, father of philosopher Vedran from the 'round table'. A dissident Serb, member of the Communist Alliance before the war, he used to work as a metallurgist at mines throughout the region. He had been sentenced to death because he persisted in warning about the pernicious consequences of nationalism. He traced the roots of the particular criminal activity in Prijedor to the Second World War and a particular moment in the history of anti-fascist partisans. He described how Prijedor had been a symbol of coexistence, Serbs, Croats and Bosniaks fighting together against the Nazi invaders. During that war, he told us, the Serbs were punished the most severely, shot or taken in large numbers to the nearby concentration camp of Jasenovac while the Bosniaks and Croats were driven out of their homes but mostly escaped being killed. He explained that this discrimination driving a wedge between the ethnic communities had the intended effect of weakening opposition: divide and rule. The policy caused a fatal rift between these communities and this wound festered throughout the decades of communism which, for political rather than humanitarian reasons, put a lid on inter-ethnic grudges. However at the collapse of Communism the suppressed Serb desire for revenge and retribution against Bosniaks and Croats, perceived as having been traitors and collaborators, burst its dam. The Bosnia War broke out.

'Coexistence requires truth,' Mladen Grahovac told us, 'but the truth has to be for all three parties concerned equally. Otherwise there will be war again in the future. The international community is responsible for the current situation because war perpetrators tailored the post-war peace and established the political parties now running the country. Prijedor is worse than Srebrenica because in Srebrenica the crimes were committed by the militia in one offensive. In Prijedor the process continued throughout the war, forty three thousand being driven out and up to four thousand killed. I went to Srebrenica in 2002 and 2003. I went to pay my respects at all the killing camps, the only Serb to do so, because I believe in the concept of reconciliation.'

He explained how religion embittered the issues of ethnicity, and politics muddied the already turbulent waters with deals made between Croats and Serbs at the expense of Bosniaks. Bosnia remained a country of different ethnic groups and these had to live together.

Mladen Grahovac gave us a wider picture of recent history than we had so far heard: the attempt by Croatia and Serbia to divide and demolish Bosnia. 'They were taking over this medieval kingdom.' Long before the war people knew blood would be spilt because of the developing unholy alliance between religion and nationalism, both repressed for decades under Communism. Nationalists and the Orthodox Church achieved their goal, and the Dayton Accord which ended the war helped create the Republika Srpska. The Kozara Memorial reflected this change. From being a monument to anti-fascism it now celebrated extreme Serb nationalism. During the Second World War the mostly Serb partisans, lead by Croat Marshal Tito, included Bosniaks, Jews and Croats. The partisan leaders realized the importance of inter-ethnicity among the troops, strength in unity. A number of nationalist Serbs left the partisans in protest at this policy. Now these Serbs had reclaimed the monument for their own purposes.

Bishop Jefrem of Banja Luka found himself in alliance with Radovan Karadjic and in June 1992 gave a lecture in front of a large audience in the city theatre announcing that it was the Serb's sacred duty to stop radical Islam with weapons. Maybe he had been ordered to say this, or perhaps he really meant it, though it was well known that Bosnian Islam not only had the reputation of being liberal and Western friendly, but in fact could be relied on to help stem the tide of radical Islam. In the event, the Bosnia War drew radical Muslims, the Mujaheddin, to a region where they had never been, nor would have ever been made welcome.

The unique character of Bosnia is its blend of ethnicity. As in Nazi Germany where the bonds and generations of intermarriage between Jews and Aryans culminated in the most virulent manifestations of anti-Semitism and eventually the Holocaust, so the close intermingling of ethnic groups and religions in the former Yugoslavia for similar reasons led to the concentration camps of Omarska, Trnopolje and Keraterm.

Mladen Grahovac a Serb married to a Bosniak, finally declared: 'Without mixing we can't make progress.'

The night before the first meeting with the miners of Omarska and the mixed group from the 'round table' we were invited for supper at Zoran's parents, a Serb married to a Croat. This was the first time we had been welcomed unofficially to a Serb household. Zoran's smiling mother, strong, stoical and pillar-like, and his petite feisty sister, Bojana, a teacher of English, had together prepared a feast of tomato soup, deep fried chicken pieces, mince meat patties, and pepper salads all piled on large platters. The women were the only earners in the family, the father unable to find employment because he had married a Croat. Our embarrassment at being given such lavish hospitality by people who barely earned enough to survive was mitigated by the fact we were employing Zoran. At supper we learned about the family's flight from the Krajina in Croatia, and the dangerous journey back to

Prijedor where the parents had married years earlier. The front line of battle followed them all the way, and the children ducked bullets. Bosniaks, Croats and Serbs sat round the table, talking about the past and the future, clinking glasses. As we left Anel and Zoran looked intently at each other and clapped the palms of their hands like team players about to start a match, or celebrating the first goal.

MINERS AND YOUNG PEOPLE

The group of miners sat in a semi-circle, truculent and defensive, looking at us sadly. Instead of beating politely about the bush we immediately told them what happened in Omarska.

'Nothing happened here,' an elderly man responded proudly. 'It was an investigation centre to root out terrorists. It was not a concentration camp. You can only call it that if there is barbed wire. There was no barbed wire here anywhere.'

The rest of them agreed, their views ranging from Omarska functioning as some kind of holiday camp for Bosniaks while they prepared to emigrate, to the mine being a place where maybe a few bad things did happen. Two of the miners had seen us at the Omarska Church ceremony and expressed relief we were not anti-Serb, but nonetheless they resisted our reading of events. They saw no need for a memorial, claiming such a monument would be provocative and whatever we built there would certainly need 24/7 protection from the miners. And anyway why weren't we building memorials to innocent Serb victims at Sarajevo?

Then Zoran spoke, quietly but with an intensity that made everyone hold their breath: 'I am a Serb. This place was a black hole. What happened here besmirches me.'

Suddenly the floodgates opened. All the miners shouted and gesticulated: 'You call yourself a Serb! Don't you realize that if we hadn't killed the Muslims they would have killed you!'

The truth had been spoken and acknowledged. So the place had not been a holiday camp. A flimsy dressing had been ripped off revealing a wound, still suppurating, deep and wide as a crevasse.

The young members of the 'round table' looked on in shocked

silence. The conversation among the miners became animated, all of them wanting and needing to speak, pouring out a welter of comments. We put a break on these outbursts by 'reflecting back' to each speaker what they had just spoken: 'So you are saying nothing happened here, that there should be no memorial, etc...' Each time the speaker listened, nodding assent, but more half-heartedly as though slowly becoming aware of the enormity of their false assertions, that maybe things were not as they had said, yet unable to change their mind, at least not immediately.

The miners and the young people agreed to meet again, and even that there should be Bosniaks in the group (the miners not having taken on board that Anel and Emir were Bosniak). The oppressive atmosphere earlier had lifted as though all felt liberated. They shook our hands warmly, eyes brimming with emotion, and looked forward to seeing us again. They had been listened to and we had shown them respect. One of them even admitted to us sorrowfully how bad he felt when visitors came to lay flowers at the white house and stared contemptuously at him. 'But I had done nothing wrong,' he sighed.

A mild young man next to him told us how he had been one of the cooks at the Omarska church celebration. The workers' union leader, a cousin of our driver Misha, remained doubtful and non-committal, but agreed to carry on the process. However his deputy, a soldier for Karadjic, moustache bristling, sneering loudly while we spoke, eyes hooded and refusing to look directly at us, categorically insisted on a memorial for Serbs at Sarajevo. Zoran's words had made him look up for the first time, surprised and shaken; but his anger warned us to be careful.

Hatred and suspicion of Bosniaks still raged in these people. They complained about the Bosniaks being privileged and wealthy, that they returned from abroad bringing loads of cash, driving expensive cars, building large homes while Serbs remained poor. It must have been galling for these workers that the ethnic cleansing had not been successfully accomplished. What had the war been for? Now, despite being in charge of the country, they felt like an underclass, and the very people they had tried to get rid of were returning, reclaiming their land and property, demanding rights and justice and most upsetting of all to the impoverished Serbs, apparently 'rolling in money'. The miners even described Kozarac as 'millionaire's row.' One of them declared: 'They should be grateful we drove them out, they became rich!'

The 'round table' members present were shocked by this level of denial, especially at the notion that the camp had only been a collection centre. Only Sasha Drakulic, audibly seething next to me throughout the meeting, felt able to speak, challenging the miners as to why they should feel offended by having a memorial. Zoran, dressed smartly in a jacket with leather elbow pads, refused to enter the argument. He had said his piece and sat still, eyes dark with fury, his manner contained and steely. Philosopher Vedran could barely hold back tears and afterwards told us that shock prevented him saying anything. 'I had a headache.' Anel looked uncomfortable as well he might, his eyes filling and lips creased down tightly. This meeting must have been excruciating for him and he commented later that we would have to be careful what Bosniaks we brought to another encounter with the miners because: 'they might be too upset at hearing so many denials and lies.' He was thinking especially of the women survivors who had lost husbands and sons at Omarska.

There are ways of handling extremists. Let them speak, hear them out and ignore them, without entering into fruitless argument. Democratic societies permit poisonous views without suppressing freedom of speech. The art was to deflect conversations to the issue of Prijedor's perception of Omarska. Improved relations between the town and the mine, by opening a visitor's centre for instance, would widen people's perspective about what goes on there, inform them of its history, and eventually facilitate discussions about memorials.

When the young 'round table' members drove back to Prijedor they had an accident in the car, someone tried to run them off the road. Later Katerina Panic informed us she had been told they were 'marked'.

THE KILLING FIELDS OF HAMBARENE

Jasmina Devic had set up the first returnee association of women to register in the region, single women and mothers who lost children and family members in the war. The organization was based in the villages around Hambarene on the left bank of the Sana beyond Prijedor.

She spoke: 'There were thirteen thousand Bosniaks living in this region before the war. Between May and September in 1992 large numbers were killed, ethnically cleansed, homes cleared out. On July 20th about a thousand, mostly men, vanished, killed or taken away, on one day alone. Serbs from neighbouring villages killed them on the streets outside their victims' homes. They were killed because they were Muslim men. Others they took away and put in camps. Twenty two members of my family were killed. The bodies of two of my brothers were found in a mass grave. The remains of others are presumed to be in Tomasica or in the Ljubija mines. Serbs tried to hide traces of where bodies still are. In Hambarene four hundred people disappeared and only a hundred and fifty bodies have been found. I am still looking for my husband, uncles and the husbands of my sisters. Because innocent people died we do have to provide a memorial, and the best place is where they were actually killed: a sign to wake the conscience of people, everybody, to prevent it happening again. Everybody loses; even those who did the killing lost and gained nothing.'

Jasmina Devic, slender and beautiful, spoke quietly, the tone of her voice bleached of emotion, blonde hair framing a face drained of all expression, beyond sorrow and anger.

'Now about five thousand people live in the region, most returnees. We have contact with Serb women, but are not certain whether they will be prepared to talk about these issues. They are not indifferent. It is a painful past for them too. They protect their emotions in silence. Not a single man in Prijedor failed to participate in the ethnic cleansing. Between May 20th and July 22nd every man carried a gun.'

We sat listening to her story. Emir was barely able to translate, sometimes choking as he had done before at Omarska.

'I was a health worker,' Jasmina Devic continued in a quiet steady tone. 'I could see everything. I had to show up at work in Prijedor everyday. From here to my work I was searched twelve times before I got there. I saw my colleagues wearing guns and uniforms. I could simply not believe what was going on. The Serb women were also afraid.'

Jasmina Devic said she would try and bring Bosniak and Serb women together for a meeting. 'It's a necessary process. We cooperate with Serbs and get on well, but never talk about these painful issues, such as the white house.' We suggested that we simply introduce ourselves at the meeting and see how it developed.

The window of Jasmina Devic's office looked out on to an expanse of rolling hills, forests, farmsteads and meadows full of flowers all bathed in bright May sunlight. Hard to imagine this landscape had been the setting of a massacre.

Jasmina continued: 'When I was thrown out of my new home, my husband had just finished building it, and I was taken with my two children, two and four years old, to Trnopolje. I set myself an objective: I will be back! I spent five years in Germany and took the first chance to come home, first to Sanski Most in the Federation. Being a qualified midwife I could work in Germany and in Sanski Most. But they were not my home, even though it was safer to bring up my children there. I was the first returnee in 1999. My children are sixteen and seventeen years old and now go to Middle School in Prijedor, the only Bosniaks there. They are the biggest heroes. They have no father; they sit with people whose parents killed him. So far there are no problems for them. Ever since the war broke out I set myself tasks, the main one being to create normal living conditions for all of us.'

She considered our initiative to be important in bringing young Bosniaks and Serbs together because they were not used to mixing. Bosniaks still suffered from discrimination and had no work opportunities. 'The authorities in Prijedor are planning a black and white world. You must invite young Serbs to take part in this project. The young have been traumatized on both sides. It is still impossible to forget or forgive.'

We fixed a meeting of Serb and Bosniak women for our July visit, to give Jasmina Devic time. After hearing her devastating story we could not simply leave on a hand-shake and so we spent some minutes silently together. Jasmina held her hands cupped open. The room was bathed in sunlight.

Later that day in Hamborene an even hotter sun beat down on crowds of Bosniaks gathered on the killing fields overlooking Prijedor and the Vale of Kozara to remember the massacre of July 20th. Sheer numbers made the people defiant rather than depressed. Names of the dead were recited in a long list, called out in ringing tones over the heads of veiled girls sheltering under acacia trees, elderly women in hijabs squatting on the ground, families huddled in groups. The names echoed over the surrounding hills and valleys.

Then followed chants to the fallen heroes ('sehid') and white birds: 'Where are you?' and a service for those who survived presided over by Mufti Hasan Makic from Bihac. Mufti Makic was a survivor from Omarska. Azra Pasalic, the Speaker of the Municipal Assembly, reminded everyone how it had been and suddenly a ripple of laughter passed through the crowd. She had read out and waved a letter from Mayor Marko Pavic, saying he could not be present. 'He's always busy!' they muttered sarcastically. Muharem Murselevic then addressed them saying that the dead were not recognized by the Serb authorities as 'victims'. This was a denial of genocide and his voice rising to a shout he demanded justice: 'Find and punish the criminals!'

Izvor, the organization concerned with finding missing people and caring for their families, had arranged an exhibition: photos of mass graves, skulls, burials and a composite poster of the killers tried and convicted at the Hague Tribunal. These pictures told the truth. Like the exhibition at the Kozara Monument, they had the effect of inflaming anger. There would be no peace for the dead but war in the future.

Bosniak returnees packed Corda's restaurant. Summer was the busiest time of the year there. They sat outside under parasols and overlooked the street. Burly men thumped the tables, laughed loudly, their wives cackling, all seeming to shout at passing Serbs: 'We are here! We are back! Watch out!'

I had seen this attitude before. In the 1960's Israelis told me in defiant response to my dismay at Palestinian refugee camps along the Lebanese and Jordanian borders: 'We suffered! No one will hurt us again! No one will drive us from our homes. No one protected us, so now we will protect ourselves!'

The truculence of returnees indicated a shift in the region's demography and politics. Bosniaks no longer saw themselves as victims. They shared Kemal Pervanic's brother Kasim's determination not to be persecuted and if necessary to fight. The Serbs now had reason to be fearful.

Jasmina Devic failed to persuade any Serb women to attend the meeting we had planned. Instead we found ourselves facing a group of returnees, mostly men, who seemed intent on a fight. They had critized her for talking to us, none of them wanting any dealings with representatives from the Serb owned mine. She hoped we would explain the purpose of our mediation and talk about the memorial to allay their suspicions. As with the meeting with the miners, we brought along members of the 'round table'. These being mostly young Serbs, they presented an opportunity for both sides to listen to each other.

The meeting started as with the miners, the men looking grim and defensive. We tried to lighten the mood by telling a joke about the dogs barking through the night outside our hotel in Banja Luka. Three dogs regularly engaged in a noisy nocturnal conversation and they seemed to us to represent the three communities, a Serb, a Croat and a Bosniak dog yapping at each other, all three eventually being silenced by a ferocious deep growl from the international community. No one laughed.

Having explained our purpose, we broke the meeting up into groups, so the men could talk to the young Serbs from the 'round table'. The atmosphere improved markedly as the survivors realized they were being taken seriously. Katerina Panic and Zoran Djukic met Mirsad Duratevic and listened to his story, the first time either had heard in personal detail what had been kept from them for years. Both admitted to being shattered at hearing the truth.

Mirsad Duratovic, slender and good looking, reserved, smartly dressed and clutching a bunch of keys, recounted his history, a catalogue of horrors, quietly and without emotion. He had survived the white house, one of the two survivors we met to have done so, the other being Rezak Hukanovic.

'I was seventeen years old when they took me to the white house,' Mirsad told the group. 'Then they transferred me to another building, interrogated and tortured me. They beat me in three places, in the canteen, the white house and offices. The torturer will soon be on trial at the Hague Tribunal. They did not kill me because of my age, but also because my torturer was my teacher at High School. He gave me food and saved my life by hiding me in a garage where trucks were kept. But my friends were not spared. They had no protectors. I was then sent to Manjaca, another holding camp, for a short time, being hidden from the International Red Cross and then transferred to Trnopolje where after a long stay the International Red Cross eventually rescued me. My father and fifteen year old brother and ten other members of my family were killed.'

'Why did they take a seventeen year old to the white house?' he continued. 'There were two categories of prisoners and two standard sets of questions: was I a member of the defence force, did I possess a gun? And what politicians did I know, how much money did I have and what members of my family were known to be influential members of the Bosniak community? Families hid from Serbs in house basements but were flushed out and the men and women separated, the older men taken into the woods and executed. Young men would be taken to Omarska as a living shield to protect the Serbs driving them from being attacked. Neighbours and cousins were there, all of them killed. I am the only male in the family who survived.'

Mirsad Duratovic's words shocked the young Serbs from the 'round table' who now heard for the first time what happened at

Omarska. They commented on the shocking fact that the international community turned its back on the camps as though they had never happened, so the young people might not find out what had gone on there. After the meeting Anel took Zoran and others to Sejkovac, and Kemal Pervanic on his second visit home since the war, gave them a tour of the mine, explaining what happened and where. Afterwards Zoran sat in Cordas, rigid with fury. 'How could Serbs have been so stupid to do these terrible things!' was all he could say.

It became clear to us that the other survivors at the Hambarene meeting wanted to pick a fight about the mine, thinking we were mine representatives. They complained about the injustice of all the Bosniaks being sacked, claiming there were only jobs for Serbs now, and wanted to know where their murdered relatives and friends were buried in still unidentified mass graves. When we explained our independent role as mediators, helping to prepare the way for a memorial at Omarska, they became friendlier, but insisted that at the next meeting we should bring people from the mine. With the exception of Mirsad Duratovic, the men trickled away, losing interest in the project since they no longer lived in Bosnia, having jobs and new homes in Germany, Switzerland and America, and only coming back for summer vacations.

Mirsad Duratovic seemed to be the only survivor present at the meeting, along with Jasmina Devic, who had decided to return home and make a life for their families despite tensions with Serb neighbours and obstacles set up by the local authorities to discourage them, delays in providing water, electricity and phone lines as well as refusing to repair roads.

Several older Serb men apart from the members of the 'round table' attended the meeting. They kept silent, possibly afraid to be identified, or perhaps stunned by what they were hearing and unable to contribute. But one of them, Zarko Gvozden, insisted on telling his story, having waited a long time for such an opportunity:

'It is my duty to speak about the last twelve years. I am fifty five years old and witnessed all that happened in Prijedor. I am well

known in this company. In 1992 I was conscripted by the so-called
state and given a uniform and sent on military missions. As a
soldier I had nothing to do with the camps. In fact when my
Bosniak neighbours were being evicted I tried to help them with
food etc. I did hear stories between 1992 and 1995. The authorities
stigmatized one category of Serbs as 'traitors' and 'reds' (Tito's
people, former commited communists, with limited influence). I
fought three battles, but avoided capture. I used to be a guard on
watch duty. After the end of the war my lack of support for the
nationalist cause contributed to many bad things happening to me.
I became politically involved at local and national levels, and set
myself up as candidate for the Democratic Patriotic Party; then I
became a town councillor. I began to meet returnees. There was a
wall of silence about the war. I could not even speak with
colleagues about it. Long before then, in 1993, during the war, I
had a car accident and my wife and I had been hurt. A Bosniak
physio-therapist treated me. When I met him again in 1998 I made
a point of greeting him. But my example was not followed by
others. There is an extreme polarity in the Municipal Assembly.
My more liberal party got too few votes to win any seats. I went to
Sarajevo and met Lagumdzija (a Bosniak politician), who had re-
established the Social Democratic Party. When I returned home,
my compatriots in Prijedor called me a traitor and a dog. Then
sixteen months ago a Serb murdered my son. This criminal is still
at large. So I know what pain is and need to talk about it. For what
I failed to do because I did not know, I apologize and I want to be
included in any project that helps the situation improve here.'

Having got this off his chest, Zarko Gvozden attended several
further meetings, was always friendly and offered us hospitality at
the pub he ran (opposite the Metropolitan Café owned by extreme
Serb nationalists, and considering his reputation we wondered
why they had not attacked his place). However, when the issue of
the memorial began to dominate meetings he made excuses or just
failed to turn up.

The meeting at Hambarene divided into groups of Bosniak men
and young Serbs from the 'round table'. They spoke freely,

highlighted significant issues and produced a series of proposals.

First they agreed that all sites needed to be honoured, marking those places that had been killing camps and also where bones were found, not just Omarska. Secondly, people needed to learn about the ideological movements that lead to genocide and to understand the mechanisms used to instigate the process of ethnic cleansing. People who have lived as close neighbours for generations do not usually hate each other; mutual suspicion is politically manipulated. Thirdly, justice must be a priority. Once war criminals are extracted from the community, Serbs can begin to unburden themselves of guilt and feel liberated from their dark past so the situation may have a chance of improving. Denial and the wall of silence create morbidity.

Everyone expressed disappointment with their own ethnic group and came to the conclusion that employment would be the first step to bringing people together. Working and talking side by side. Mirsad Duratovic as secretary of his local community, the neighbouring village of Biscani, had found a German donor after a four year search to help rebuild the school. The conditions were that a Serb and a Bosniak company had to work together on this project. Despite mutual suspicions and continuing hatred by Serbs for Bosniak returnees, they cooperated on this multi-ethnic project. It functioned because everyone needed work.

One of the groups at the meeting raised the issue of people being victims of political systems. Ethnic groups should not hate each other. What mattered in the next years to come was creating a climate where Serbs could condemn the murderers. They agreed that working together would tear down the wall of silence: two men operating the same machine will learn to solve life's problems collectively. This raised the issue of employment at the mine. All the Bosniaks at the meeting had worked there before being made redundant when the war started. They demanded reinstatement.

Mirsad Duratovic's story had so appalled the Serbs at the meeting that they insisted on truth being a major issue for the future. People's stories had to be heard, documented and recorded. Finding bodies was another priority.

'Two hundred and fifty people from my village are still not located. I don't even know where many of my family members are, though I can only assume they were killed,' said Mirsad Duratovic, continuing: 'All the things we proposed at this meeting must happen. Political obstruction comes from all three communities, not just the Serbs. You have come to Hambarene, but the international community supported those powers who committed the crimes in the first place. So there is no progress. The international community knows what to do. It provided a memorial at Srebrenica but forgot about what happened in other places, even worse crimes. They play with our feelings. The view of most poorly educated people here is that the international community patronizes them. They also see how much money the international community earns here. The gap in wages between foreigners and Bosnians is immense.'

The meeting ended with only Jasmina Devic, Mirsad Duratovic and the young Serbs committed to the process. The 'round table' gathered at Cordas and talked about memorials not being sufficient. Mass graves had to be identified, the rest of the missing bodies found and all Serbs who had committed crimes be brought to justice.

'I am a Serb, I did nothing wrong,' said Sasha Drakulic. 'Why should I be made to pay for what others did?'

Anel felt positive: 'The meeting was good. People talked openly, especially in the groups. Young and old mixed together. This was the first time for many.'

THREATS

Mayor Marko Pavic smiled and looked straight at us as he shook our hands. We were struck by the intense pale blueness of his eyes.

We told him about our meetings with the mine workers and the survivors at Hambarene, and how both groups agreed to meet each other. We proposed a visitor's centre at the mine, consisting of a technology museum where the white house could be an oasis of peace and a memorial of what happened during the war. Living memorials like this would transform Prijedor and the way the outside world perceived this 'black hole'.

The mayor listened and seemed better disposed to us than at our first meeting. He could not yet make up his mind whether we were just a couple of fools whom he could ignore or whether our presence and activities might stir up a threat to his invincible position as Godfather of Prijedor. Seeing us regularly meant he could monitor our progress and also be seen by the international community as being co-operative. He had so far successfully persuaded them of his sympathetic nature: a man they could do business with and who would be our ally.

We also knew he could stop the project whenever he liked.

'Thank you for this proposal,' he said, continuing to smile, making us think of a crocodile about to open his massively grinning jaws before devouring us. 'I am a man to do everything possible for reconciliation and the betterment of life in my town. I am not a person to shirk responsibilities and therefore am extremely interested in this project. I am aware of everything that happened, of multi-ethnicity and all things of importance. I met with your boss, the chief executive of the mine's new owners. He came for a visit and sat where you are now. But we only talked about business. We did not touch on any of these issues.'

The mayor laid his trump cards on the table preparing to deliver a mortal blow to our work. He needed to let us know that the mine owners and the international community supported him.

'Two parts of your project are good to my mind. Improving relations between the mine and Prijedor and presenting a good image of the town to the world. But the part about joint meetings between Serbs and Bosniaks to decide on a memorial I don't accept. You won't get the town council's agreement. They alone should decide about the white house. But I can tell you that there can be no reconciliation between the mine and a memorial.'

Initially we assumed he had not understood our proposal about the visitor's centre being of benefit to Omarska and the whole region: a museum that included a memorial which people could visit if they chose, but whose chief purpose was to explain the workings of the mine. As the months of our project went by we realized this misconception suited Mayor Pavic. He persisted in calling the visitor's centre a memorial centre, despite our attempts to correct him, and he ignored the perspective of the project which wanted the acknowledgement of the crime implicit in the memorial to be a significant part of Prijedor's renaissance. He remained opposed to a memorial of any sort, would not be budged on this issue even by the Office of the High Representative or the mine owners, and tried to block our progress at every turn.

Still smiling amicably and looking at us through the impenetrable cerulean blue of his irises he continued to dismantle our process: 'Lies led the mine owners to send you here, scurrilous articles in Dani.' Dani was a well respected Bosnian weekly published in Sarajevo. 'The mine was not a concentration camp and you will find no bodies there. Prijedor will support the mine's new owners. The company helps makes this town prosperous. Nothing will disrupt the cooperative relationship between them and Prijedor. But if the mine owners decide to turn the white house into a memorial they will not have the support of the town council. Your memorial centre will give Prijedor a bad name, and we will not allow that.'

He then repeated the mantras he recited to us on our first visit and to all visitors from abroad: firstly, Prijedor was the first town in the whole of Bosnia to allow returnees and secondly, Serbs were not being allowed to put up plaques in the Federation. He concluded: 'No reconciliation can happen. Bosnia is not ready for that; it needs time, generations and years.'

Realizing he may have gone too far, and that we resisted his attempts to kill the project he added grudgingly: 'Drawings of the memorial centre may help. If I approve of them then perhaps the town council can see them. And we should continue talking.' He would certainly not approve of any drawings, whatever we came up with, and the idea of delay suited him. While he ran Prijedor he did not want any discussion about what happened in the war. But his door remained open to us for him to make sure our project failed.

These meetings may have been a charade, but they provided us with a unique opportunity to study a significant Bosnian politician.

Our project then hit the buffers from two opposing positions: the mayor on the Serb side, and Edin Ramulic from the organization Izvor on the Bosniak side. Mayor Pavic had no more implacable enemy than Edin Ramulic whom we visited next. However both were united in their opposition to the project, but for different reasons. Mayor Pavic's constituency consistenly refused to acknowledge what happened in Omarska, whereas Edin Ramulic represented a vociferous Bosniak opinion that the mine should be closed and the whole area be turned into a memorial.

Edin Ramulic lived in Sanski Most, the nearest town to Prijedor but securely in the Federation and he commuted to the Izvor office in Prijedor when needed. The rest of the time he ran an internet café in Sanski Most, which gave him opportunity whenever he wanted to report to the worldwide diaspora of Bosniaks about our activities.

We made a serious miscalculation at this meeting. In our enthusiasm to get the memorial discussed we inadvertently rushed our fences with the one group of people whom we felt would be most sympathetic. We underestimated the divisions in the Bosniak community, specifically between those who lived in Prijedor and those who lived elsewhere, either in the Federation or abroad.

The Guardian journalist Ed Vulliamy and Edin Ramulic had together ducked Serb bullets as they fled through the hills of Northern Bosnia during the war. Edin lost many members of his family and his face had become a fist of anger.

Izvor operated from an office paid for by the Prijedor town council, a fact that raised questions in the Bosniak community of Prijedor as to the precise relationship of this organization with the Serb authorities. The Serb authorities provided the premises but limited the political scope of Izvor's activities.

At first Edin Ramulic spoke co-operatively, though his glowering eyes should have warned us of danger. At first we thought a recent break-in and stolen fax machine had upset him, but gradually we realized he resented our presence and methods.

For all his antagonism to us we had to remember the trauma he had suffered personally, and also the incalculable effect of constantly working with human remains and grief-stricken families.

'It is complicated,' he responded to our question about Izvor's work. 'We are involved in matters that should never have happened: re-exhumation. Before DNA it was not possible to identify bodies, so they were buried no-one knowing who they were. Now we have to prepare blueprints for burial sites, digging them up again. The worst is we have no clear numbers. The authorities in the Republika Srpska paid no attention to orderly procedures, unlike the Federation. There were about two hundred bodies in the latest mass grave to be found. It took fifteen days to locate their position precisely, fifteen bodies in one place, all in a mess and unmarked. They had not been buried properly, so gathering the remains was expensive and upsetting. So much work needs to be done on re-exhumation that finding other mass graves has to be postponed. No organization is in charge, just local religious communities and community representatives, but no one taking over-all responsibility.'

The meeting began in a calm atmosphere of giving us important information. But gradually he became impatient at having to repeat grisly facts. He pursed his lips and then continued, his scowl become ever more intense: 'There are so many anniversaries being marked now. Apart from the one you came to in Hambarene, on 20th July, there is the annual visit to Keraterm on the 24th and to Omarska on 6th August. Then on 21st August there is the visit to Mount Vlasic, site of a mass execution. There is also no coordinator of support networks for the courts. Apart from that we have to rebuild trust in the judiciary system. It is important to identify perpetrators as well as victims. The International Council for Missing Persons (ICMP) supports with financial expenses. Everyone involved has missing relatives, husbands, sisters etc. Because I run a cyber café with assistants I have free time to spend helping. There are still one thousand and four hundred bodies missing. Lack of information prevents them being found. Bosniak survivors and eyewitnesses sometimes come forward, and sometimes a mass grave is found by accident. The mines are the only locations we cannot get information. Those who buried the bodies don't want to come forward. We need help from the State or from international agencies to use radar or aerial photography.'

'We have a concrete proposal,' he went on, in barely controlled fury. 'The main problem is lack of information. Local Serbs must tell us where the graves are. For instance recently a Serb agreed to reveal the location of a pit not far from Bosanska Krupa in exchange for having his roof repaired. We need to extract this information discreetly, without involving the police. We have to strike bargains with indictees at the Hague Tribunal. There are legal procedures to follow, but court proceedings are being moved from The Hague to Sarajevo and other local principalities where the crimes took place. However there is the danger that we will meet obstacles from those authorities which are not interested in pursuing justice.'

Edin Ramulic correctly identified the fundamental problem that had to be solved before people could even begin to think of memorials: finding missing bodies, identifying the killers and bringing them to justice. Where were the missing bodies? Until this question could be answered the issue would continue to burn and there could be little possibility of reconciliation or discussion about memorials.

Moreover the half-hearted attempts by the international community to catch the two main war criminals, Radovan Karadjic and General Mladic, left Bosniaks cynical and sceptical, giving rise to conspiracy theories and Bosniak suspicions of the international community's motives.

From what Edin was telling us, it seemed as though the issue could never be solved. What differentiates an issue from a problem is that the latter can find a solution, whereas the former remains a point of pain and conflict needing attention, understanding and resolution. Therefore our mediation process had to continue, and by bringing both sides together, building trust, Serbs might eventually feel able to give information.

We were entering even trickier waters than with the mayor, whose resistance to the project came from his involvement in the crime. For the Bosniak community there was unfinished business, not just concerning missing bodies, but with everything that happened in the war, giving rise to a range of feelings from grief to revenge.

At this stage of the meeting we made our miscalculation. Edin Ramulic had already warned us about it being too soon for talk of reconciliation, so we needed to tread carefully on the issue of memorials. Nevertheless we wanted to start conversations about the ultimate objective of our project and began to share ideas for discussion. We talked about 'living memorials' as opposed to granite monoliths, putting them in context of the mine and the communities of Omarska and Prijedor. We compounded our mistake by going on at length about the mine and corporate responsibility, an issue which could not have been of less interest to Izvor. Edin Ramulic had now been joined by Seida Karabasic, whom we met on a previous visit and who had explained to us the gruelling responsibility of Izvor, informing relatives of dead family members being identified at Sejkovac. Seida sighed, looking into her lap, while Edin Ramulic began to fume. Disregarding their obvious discomfort we continued with a description of a visitor's centre at the mine, which along with being a museum would tell its history, including its use as a concentration camp. To cap everything we spoke about the white house being made beautiful, mines being ugly places, and the need to honour the deaths of the innocent, turning the place into an oasis of peace. As though we had not inadvertently insulted them enough we suggested a union of religious symbols of death and resurrection, Christian and Bosniak at the memorial. As an example we described the church at Presnace outside Banja Luka where a Catholic priest and nun had been murdered by Serb soldiers and which had become a shrine. In conclusion we said: 'Where innocent blood is shed is hallowed ground.'

Edin Ramulic exploded: 'This is scandalous! If you were not a religious organization I would not even talk with you and would kick you out of here.' He spluttered something Emir did not translate, so we assumed he had made an even more serious threat. 'We can not stop your project, but remember: Omarska was Auschwitz. I have been to many places of suffering all over the former Yugoslavia and never saw an oasis of peace. Bodies cry out for justice. They are not asking for oases of peace! I am here to make sure they get justice. Not vengeance, but justice! Victims need justice more than peace. We cannot be any part of your proposal. Talk to the families of victims. Listen to what they want, to what is important to them. This initiative has to be transparent and cannot be imposed. Nor can there be any religious components in the white house, and definitely not Orthodox ones. There can be no help for the Orthodox Church anyway. Read my lips: those who suffered want no religious symbols!'

He had misunderstood us, that we had only meant to offer suggestions to get people thinking about a possible memorial, but it was too late. Edin Ramulic could no longer be reasoned with. Seida Karabasic tried to calm the situation by emphasising the point about justice rather than vengeance, although Edin's manner implied the opposite. Then she too began to shake with fury. 'We can't allow you to abuse the suffering of people and the deaths of victims by creating something beautiful out of it, even for the sake of our children and their children. It is true we have to support an education which stops the hatred. Neighbours killed my father but I don't hate them...' Choking with emotion she fell silent.

'Make a place of peace in the town centre park,' Edin Ramulic suggested, 'but leave Omarska and Jasenovac for what they are.'

He rejected further discussion with us, the implication being that Izvor should be solely in charge of any memorial, and from then on he opposed our project.

The notion about an 'oasis of peace' had come from Emsuda Mujagic, and the nature of memorials as symbols of reconciliation or revenge became an issue in all discussions on the project. We told her about our run in with Edin Ramulic and asked her to explain our position to him so he remained online with us. She told us: 'He lost many members of his family in the camps. He faced

much prejudice and suffering. What was worse, he did not participate in any healing process. No wonder he is still bitter. It doesn't
surprise me he threatened you, we know him, but he wouldn't
hurt anyone!' But she did agree with him about leaving religion
out of the memorial. 'We don't want to insult victims. Religious
symbols were abused by criminals. These symbols encouraged
hatred. Leave hate out of the memorial.'

Edin Ramulic had insisted on pictures of the murderers being
prominently displayed in the white house. 'People should see the
pictures,' agreed Emsuda Mujagic. 'They must stop regarding
these criminals as heroes.' This raised the issue of what reaction
such a memorial was intended to provoke: fear, hate or pity? It did
not have the same function as a war memorial which commemo-
rated the bravery of soldiers dying for the fatherland. 'Serb
memorials are an insult to victims,' said Emsuda.'Children gather
by these war memorials and only think of Serb victims, but there
were no Serb victims like those innocent people murdered.
Soldiers cannot be regarded in the same way as innocent victims.'

Emsuda Mujagic felt that the whole mine should be a memorial,
turning the offices and punishment blocks into museums, listing
the names of all the victims, showing films, being a repository of
documentary evidence for the future. However she knew that the
mine as the chief provider of employment in the region needed to
continue working, so such a solution could only be a dream. Edin
Ramulic however wanted to close the mine down completely.
Living in Sanski Most he had no concern for the economic
prosperity of Prijedor. Most Bosniaks living in the Federation
shared the attitude of a friend of mine in Sarajevo who told us
bluntly: 'Prijedor can disappear down a black hole and be eternally
forgotten for what they did there!'

PLACES OF MURDER
KERATERM

A small plaque on the ground outside the entrance of Keraterm, a
redbrick building that had once been a tile factory, reminded
visitors that out of the hundreds imprisoned at this old tile factory

three hundred were killed. Some dead flowers lay scattered over the plaque and the grass grew tall around it. The factory was no longer operational, dust and total stillness hung over the desolate building.

On our first visit we hesitated entering the killing rooms of Trnopolje, Keraterm and Omarska, partly because we felt uneasy but also out of respect for the victims. We had accompanied survivors who recounted their stories and it felt prurient to explore the spaces where they had suffered so much. But for the sake of the memorial we needed to look closely at these places and let them speak to our imagination.

We were told by a couple of young men repairing a car on the forecourt that the director had gone on holiday, but when Anel phoned him on his mobile he appeared within minutes. Since the business had closed down, no workers on site, no production in progress, dust and cobwebs everywhere, his position as director seemed nominal. Perhaps he hoped our presence signalled interest in the business, his eyes lighting up at the mention of the new mine owners.

A map of Mount Athos decorated the wall of his office, marking all the Orthodox monasteries there. This reminded us of Emsuda Mujagic and Edin Ramulic's words about religion's inspirational role for the killers.

The director had been well primed for hard questions about Keraterm's past.

'The facts are known', he said in a cool tone as though referring to a minor incident. 'I came here first in 2002 and personally dissociate myself from the crimes. While these atrocities were taking place I was a solder on the battlefield in a difference place.' Like all the other Serbs we talked to so far, including the mayor of Prijedor, everyone seemed to have been elsewhere involved in other more noble activities. No one had been around when the killing happened. 'Muharem Murselevic requested a plaque to mark this place of suffering. I have the minutes of meetings between Izvor, the association of inmates, and the shareholders of this factory. As a manager I didn't have the authority to agree to this request, and had to defer it to the shareholders.' Who were these shareholders? The factory had long ceased to operate and work did not look about to start again, which raised questions about the viability of the business let alone non-existent profits. The director went on regardless, speaking from a well-worn script: 'The shareholders had a meeting and for technical reasons the demands could not be met. We met someone from the Office of the High Representative and had a discussion about a memorial. The shareholders gave the same reply. It is the usual tactics of Bosniak victims to run to the international community when the local authorities turn down their request. Serb survivors of the massacre in Sarajevo were outraged about the possibility of a memorial to Bosniaks here.'

'What is your personal opinion?' we asked him directly.

'Regardless of ethnicity, wherever there is suffering there should be memorials. But nothing exaggerated, all dignified and solemn. The truth will out in the fullness of time. So we agreed to the plaque, modest and placed there in a peaceful manner.'

We pressed further, prizing him away from his script, and he quickly opened up, relieved to be speaking his mind. What alarmed the shareholders was that a large memorial would deter future business partners and clients. He explained the true diffi-culties of the present situation. 'The company has stopped operating, we are going bankrupt. Money is owed to the state and to former partners. There are forty seven employees, most of them elderly whom we can't pay and who are not likely to find employment anywhere else. We survive by renting spaces to shops and wait for a good solution. A company in Belgrade is interested; also an Italian company wants to make furniture here. We have had offers to turn the place into a factory for bauxite road surfacing or for grain crushing.' We did not ask whether these companies knew about the history of Keraterm, and if so, would that be a reason for no one taking matters further?

'We always lived in peace here,' he droned on, returning to his script. 'Others caused the war. We used to defend ourselves as a community. Can we not live together again? My godfather and best man is a Bosniak. We holiday together with our wives. We have to single out and punish the idiots, those individuals who distinguished themselves in war as criminals.'

Tiring of repeating the same speech time and again he began to lose patience and suddenly scowled at us: 'I need to say something to you personally: you have problems in Northern Ireland and Spain. Go and deal with your problems first before coming to us. Forget about advising and guiding us, leave us alone to sort our situation.' He added threateningly: 'Only then will relations improve locally.' He implied that the Serbs could then complete the ethnic cleansing undisturbed by international interference. Absence of Bosniaks meant no need for memorials. He then attacked the West, America mainly, for its patronizing attitudes and not understanding places like Bosnia. 'Superior wealth doesn't entitle you to tell the rest of the world what to do.'

We took his criticism, not wanting to aggravate him further, realizing from our experience of earlier interviews with Serbs the futility of argument. We agreed however on the fact that a small percent of criminals had succeeded in imposing their murderous policies on the larger passive proportion of the whole population. Like so many older Serbs in Bosnia still living in the past of their parents and grandparents he blamed the Germans for this. This reminded us of the divide and rule tactics the Nazis employed in all the territories they had invaded, a traumatic legacy from the Second World War, and a significant factor of the Bosnia War ignored or underestimated by the international community.

The German link dominated our tour of the factory. A gigantic Nurnberg Riedhammer gas oven loomed at the centre of the vast empty workshop. It had been installed during the Second World War. The doors with domed tops, large handles and bolts, familiar from photos of Auschwitz, had shut on tiles not bodies, but reminded us of other ethnic massacres.

We inspected the rooms where these had taken place, spaces now emptied of all furniture, cleaned up and showing no trace of what happened. Dust settled.

The memorial museum demanded by the survivors might find a perfect location here, once the shareholders realized they would not find someone to buy the business or become partners. The factory stood on the edge of town, accessible to all who wanted to visit and large enough to house a whole century of evidence, films and literature about this particular region of Europe: a history of conquests, betrayals and retributions involving all the ethnic groups and their manipulation by international politics attempting to control this fault line between the Christian West and the Islamic East.

TRNOPOLJE

The ruined old school house at Trnopolje already stood as a memorial to the torture, rape and murder of women and children incarcerated there during the first year of the Bosnia War. Unlike the insignificant looking white house at the Omarska mine, the crumbling walls and gaping window spaces of this relatively impressive building possessed a broken dignity that spoke of violation. A slogan in praise of Tito still decorated an interior wall in large brightly painted letters. The words no longer looked down on rows of obedient communist children but a rubble strewn floor where weeds and shrubs had already taken vigorous hold. The place in itself represented a century of history. A rudimentary knowledge of what happened there sufficed to explain the unresolved community tensions of the whole region. On one side stood the new school attended by exclusively Serb children who might or might not know its history. On the other side the local authorities had raised a memorial to Serb soldiers who died for a Greater Serbia in the Bosnia War. On the opposite side of the road a local Serb businessman had built an ostentatiously expensive house on land where once stood a hut used by police and passing soldiers for interrogation purposes and the regular rape of Bosniak girls picked out from the women held prisoner in the old school house.

No plaque or description yet explained this place. The international community closed the camp in 1992 and left it as it was.

Trnopolje recalled the ruins of Birkenau, a couple of miles outside Auschwitz, where the long sheds, chimneys and watch-towers are allowed over time to gradually crumble and be swallowed by the ground.

In Birkenau children from the town and neighbouring villages now play hide and seek in the sheds on Sunday strolls with their parents and school groups are taken on tours, teenagers wearing ear phones, texting or chatting on their mobiles as they march oblivious along the rail track that enters the wide expanse of the former concentration camp under the gate-house, the only familiar landmark unmistakeable from countless photos and films. Nothing in the otherwise desolate flatness of fields and ditches flanked in the distance by a small birch wood speaks to these visitors as there is only the most cursory information in several languages to be read on the walls of the entrance about the hundreds of thousands killed there.

The intention is to allow history to disappear until the area becomes a flat field and future generations will not know what happened. This policy raises questions about memory and marking the deaths of innocent victims. The Russians who liberated Auschwitz and took responsibility for preserving the place probably did not want to draw attention to their own concentration camps, a chain of gulags across the former Soviet Union. But shame attaches to all humanity for a crime that was allowed to happen. Killed victims cannot remember and survivors will die within a few generations, so demands for a memorial that does justice to the horror of what happened can be allowed to rage in the knowledge that the passing of time will dim the sound, just as the ground gradually swallows the evidence.

OMARSKA: THE WHITE HOUSE

The white house once built as a temporary shelter from the rain for workers already showed signs of deterioration and if left the flimsy walls and roof would eventually fall down.

The security officer handed us keys to the building with a friendly smile. After the meeting with the union members, word had gone round we were fair-minded.

The interior looked as ordinary as the outside: two rooms on each side of a small passage with a gutted shower and toilet ahead of the entrance. The first room on the left had empty shelves and an old television set. The others were empty. Windows on one side looked out over a large meadow shimmering under a fierce summer sun, the grasses and flowers drying out. Beyond it villagers tended cattle and made hay. In the distance Mount Kozara rose over thick woods. On the other side the view was dominated by the mine, red brick walls of the big hangar rearing up to a row of office windows where throughout their incarceration in the offices prisoners were warned not to look out or they would be killed. Kemal Pervanic's brother Kasim dared to do so and observed the activities in the white house, people being marched in and bodies being thrown out.

The white house stood between nature and the mine, a timeless landscape on the one hand and industrial activity on the other.

It made sense to preserve the building as a memorial: a place of no words. The smallness of the white house meant it could not be used as a museum. We considered a book of memory with the names of victims. This would have to be encased on a lectern in the entrance. Information or panels would only clutter the walls. A sculpture could be placed in each room. We wanted to present the survivors with ideas to kindle their own imagination. These included the notion, rejected by survivors, of trees growing slowly over the building eventually to conceal it. They did not want the place ever hidden.

The concept of memorials to atrocities, as opposed to soldiers killed in action, was relatively new. Most concentration camps from the Second World War across Europe had been turned into museums or, as at Birkenau, been deliberately left to the ravages of time and weather, but with no intention of turning these places into anything inappropriate. The white house stood in the middle of a working mine. One of the places that used to be crowded with prisoners had been turned into a canteen. Offices where women were raped and men were interrogated tortured and killed remained offices in use. Mine machinery now moved in and out of the hangar where the prisoners once witnessed atrocities.

Only the white house remained unused, a reminder to the workers of what happened. They probably preferred it to be taken away, but the new mine owners had decreed it must not be touched. No one had vandalised the building, no insults scrawled on the walls, no broken windows. It seemed that despite their denials of anything criminal taking place there, the workers had a superstitious respect for the building, knowing that something so awful happened inside that anyone going near or defacing it might be cursed.

GUILT AND SHAME

'You have to meet murderers!' insisted Sasha Drakulic from the 'round table'.

He disapproved of Anel and Zoran's control of our agenda, since they arranged meetings with mainly members of the Murselovic clan and those Serbs whom he considered to be peripheral in the war, because they did not participate in any crimes.

Mayor Milomir Stakic and his cronies had provided the environment for the murderers to pursue their crimes unhampered. But no one we talked with admitted to even being in Prijedor during that time. They had fought as soldiers in other parts of Bosnia, or just been elsewhere. All these Serbs protested their innocence or ignorance until we met Boris Danovic. Sasha Drakulic overruled our project managers' reluctance concerning this man; they felt that his guilt would make him of little use to the project.

Boris Danovic had been director of the Omarska mine during the time the place had been used as a killing camp from May to August 1992. He had intimate knowledge of the mine and the mine manager valued his experience, which explained why he still worked there.

Boris Danovic immediately surprised us with a warmer greeting than we received from any other Serb we had yet met at the mine. He spoke openly about his part in the war, and as the conversation continued seemed to want to unburden himself of a heavy history.

'I gave testimony at the Hague Tribunal in defence of the mayor of Prijedor,' he began, referring not to Marko Pavic but to Milomir Stakic, who had been Kemal Pervanic's dentist only days before sending him to Omarska. Milomir Stakic was one of the first major criminals of the war to be punished and imprisoned by the Hague Tribunal. Boris Danovic did not apologize for his testimony. 'You can read it on the internet.' He wanted to speak the truth, regardless of morality or judgement on his actions.

'You have to consider all the events leading up to what happened in 1992,' he went on. 'The region was split illegally.' He was referring to the way nationalist Serbs set up a parallel administration to the legal one in Prijedor. This alternative police force gradually replaced the predominantly Bosniak one by a mixture of threats and violence, sending all non-Serb officials of the municipality who did not flee the town to the Omarska camp.

His narrative version of the Bosnia War followed. All wars are told by both sides, each knowing in intimate detail the course of events from their own perspective, the victors adding a moral gloss to make their own crimes and mistakes shine as necessary expediency for honourable victory and the losers laying the blame for failure elsewhere. War stories are among the most double-edged self-justifications of humanity on everyone's part since history began. The tragedy of wars' consequences, the intolerable suffering of innocents and the wholesale destruction of cultures remain just footnotes to violent events which societies persist in claiming to be of paramount significance.

However the double-edge of Boris's story was sharpened and made poignant by an unexpected ruefulness at what events made him do.

'Before the war began I already had an idea of what would happen and organized a peace movement with a friend,' he told us. 'This movement was headed by a Zagreb journalist. By working through that organization I tried to reconcile people throughout the region. Ordinary people wanted that. I organized meetings between the three extremist parties, the SDA (Bosniak),

HDZ (Croat) and SDS (Serb). All sent representatives except the Croats. An unholy alliance existed between the three and the conference was not successful. All towed their separate party lines. Then the Serbs took over power in March 1992. Tensions grew and snapped. At the end of April forces from outside came to power and took control.' (Boris Danovic was referring to the illegal alternative Serb controlled administration of Prijedor). 'The fear factor forced people everywhere to raise barricades. Police went out of control and from May 1992 incidents grew more violent. On May 30th paramilitary Croats and Bosniaks attacked Prijedor from the Western parts of Bosnia, Bihac and the borders with Croatia. There were many casualties and a curfew. From that moment on I could not even get to work at Omarska. On the 28th May the chief-of-police of Prijedor ordered the opening of an interrogation centre at the Omarska mine. Arrests followed and the torture and killing of Bosniaks.'

So Boris Danovic did not deny what happened, unlike the workers and other members of the mine management.

'I was helpless,' he went on. 'I wanted to free people from Omarska. A good friend of mine, a Bosniak, was taken there and I would have been happy to take his place. The police threatened to hang me. In 1991 the mine had one thousand one hundred Bosniaks working there, one thousand Croats and two thousand Serbs. There were rumours of people being killed at Omarska on the streets of Prijedor. Despite these rumours I actually saw these people alive later. Something did happen there, but I'm not sure what. The Hague Tribunal has determined the truth and perpetrators are being sentenced. I am sixty three years old and bore witness. I was called as a defence witness at the trial of Mayor Milomir Stakic and tried to answer all the questions. They even accused me of being a member of the Crisis Staff but this was disproved at the tribunal. A journalist from the Federation even accused me of being the brain behind the organization. I am suing them. The police department organized it, not me. It is necessary to mark the place where innocent people suffered and died. I am also aware that local people will oppose this. Similar crimes also occurred in Tuzla and Sarajevo against Serbs but these Serbs are forbidden to have plaques. All people should have memorials. Be warned of the fact that what you are doing in Omarska will be politicised. But this memorial must happen. I support it as long as the mine's work is not disrupted.'

'Demonization of Serbs will end when the true facts about the numbers killed are known,' he continued, aware of the work of the Hague Tribunal's brief in Bosnia coming to an end and therefore it being ever more unlikely that this truth would ever be known. 'Many Serbs died in the battle of Kozarac,' he told us, making out that the massacre of young Bosniaks on the streets of that town had been a legitimate conflict because some of the victims had the temerity to resist. These were small groups of Bosniaks trying in vain to halt the killing by attacking Serbs from the woods around Mount Kozara.

'Since the mine came under new management the crimes of Omarska have become headlines, figures are being bandied about of those tortured and killed. Bosniaks have a hidden agenda and want the mine to pay damages for crimes committed against them.'

It seemed as though Boris Danovic was reverting to being an apologist for Serb actions and we began to consider the meeting yet another failure. Nevertheless we felt he could be useful for the project because of his experience at the mine and we persisted in drawing him out. He had not expected us to be so patient and sympathetic. Suddenly he launched into a confession.

'In 1992 came the order to dismiss all Croats and Bosniaks from the work-force at Omarska. I did this. Those who failed to turn up for work when war broke out were sacked, about one thousand eight hundred of them. War raged between July and August, even though a state of war was only announced in 1995. Croats and Bosniaks did not dare come to work; so their absence gave me the opportunity to sack them. I wanted to save my family! I managed to save my son by sending him to Belgrade. I also joined the army. I am a coward. You have to know this. I was afraid for my son and the rest of my family. Relatives of friends were dying. It was chaos.

No morals. People survived as best they could.'

He did not mention what Sasha Drakulic and Katerina Panic from the 'round table' told us, that he had taken great risks to save Bosniak friends, driving them personally to safety when he could. If these facts were known his life would be in danger, still, from Serbs considering him to be a traitor.

But he did not seem afraid to be part of the project. 'I will help you of course. Tensions are still high. In the fullness of time they should calm down. The level of guilt and nationalism is a terrible burden. Dayton was the biggest error. It should have been forbidden for nationalist parties to flourish. Warmongers are still in power. They will never give up.'

TALKING TO ONE ANOTHER

RETURN TO BOSNIA: SEPTEMBER 2005

We crossed the Sava Bridge into Bosnia from Croatia and drank coffee by the edge of a busy road. Cars, trucks and buses threw up clouds of dust into the hot September air. Kate Goslett, a consultant and psycho-therapist invited to help facilitate the first conversations between Bosniaks and Serbs, needed to register and process first impressions. After the deserted flatlands and the soporific Croatia motorway by the side of which solitary ragged buzzards perched waiting for carrion killed by traffic, the sudden bustle of Bosnia always overwhelmed. Kate noted the excessive stress of daily life. Anel and Misha tensed up, agitatedly phoning on their mobiles and lighting one cigarette after the other. 'Under this thin veneer of normality,'she observed, 'anything can snap at any time and the whole place explode. Could just be an egg box falling on a man's head.'

Our meeting with Boris Danovic had concluded the first stage of the project. Within a self-imposed limited period we had met representatives from across Prijedor society and identified those who were ready to begin conversations with their enemy. We considered a lengthy process of engaging with people to be counter-productive, since the issue about the memorial demanded urgency. As foreigners we tried to avoid outstaying our welcome, or be seen to own the project. Our chief objective was to inspire and encourage the people themselves to take charge of the process. Those who criticised us, Mayor Marko Pavic most prominent, kept insisting on the necessity of getting the majority of people on our side first. They knew the impossibility of this task and hoped we would leave discouraged then there need not be a memorial. Our method relied on identifying those significant few people in the community, from all sides, who would take charge of the project. This process has been described as creating a 'critical yeast' as opposed to a 'critical mass' – not great numbers bringing about change, but a core group who influence the rest of the community.

So far women, Serb and Bosniak, young people, mostly Serb, and survivors had emerged as the best agents for this process. Now we planned initial meetings and conversations between them to ferment the yeast culture. This could then begin to react positively on the dough of Prijedor.

The night before leaving for Bosnia a dream reminded me of my past. I dreamed about a city with people under house arrest. Doors locked automatically as you entered. I approached an old house in an inner city street, a van parked outside; I knew that a guard sat silently watchful at the wheel. I stepped into an old-fashioned hallway with torn linoleum, no light, all grey with a musty smell, and climbed a flight of steps to a door. A radio played somewhere in the house and I entered a room where two people sat motionless, fearful and depressed in the dark. No words. No smiles. The radio played in another room, the only sound, entertainment bringing the outside world into this 1940's house. I recognized my grandparents. They waited for death, knowing they would soon be taken to Auschwitz. I woke up.

The world has entered a period of history when international and inter-ethnic differences continue with armed conflict but can no longer be solved by wars. Modern weapons inflict suffering grotesquely disproportionate to the causes and purposes of war. The consequent traumas last for generations of broken lives and countries, leading to more violence and destruction.

The first night at the Atina Hotel in Banja Luka I dreamed again about Auschwitz: hollow-eyed spectral figures no longer recognizable as human. They had become ciphers without feeling, beyond feeling. The words: 'It is better for them to die than continue to live,' hung in the air, unspoken. I felt ice cold; then woke up with more words sounding in my head: 'Don't forget the dead victims.'

On the way to Prijedor catalpa trees and hibiscus bloomed in gardens and corn matured from green to brown in fields. Russian vines covered hedgerows. Carpets of blue cornflowers scattered over the roadsides. Storm clouds hung over Mount Kozara.

THE FIRST MEETINGS

Three Serb women from the mine administration had agreed to meet Emsuda Mujagic and Nusreta Sivac, Bosniak women from Kozarac. Up to this moment we had seen them and everyone else individually. Our process now moved to the second stage of engineering encounters between all sides, which would culminate in the third stage of the process, a conference where decisions about the memorial would be jointly agreed.

Women seemed more positively disposed to make contact with each other. Men tended to bluster and lecture. Women were prepared to listen.

First Anel set up a meeting between his uncle, Muharem Murselevic, and Boris Danovic. They both agreed to share a drink at Le Pont, a smart Prijedor restaurant overlooking the River Sana. The hysterical croaking of masses of frogs from a nearby sluggish tributary of the Sana managed to drown out even the piped pop music. Young men leapt into the river from the bridge. Muharem Murselovic and Boris Danovic sat together but did not look at each other.

'The mine provided machinery to dig mass graves,' admitted Boris Danovic. 'Mass graves are a secondary issue, but they would have needed mine explosives.'

'I didn't count the bodies,' said Muharem Murselovic. 'But it's beyond dispute that crimes did take place.'

'Who possesses the truth?' we asked.

'We wouldn't need the Hague Tribunal if we had the truth,' said Boris Danovic. 'I am willing for all people who survived the camp to sit down with me, so I can apologize on my personal behalf.'

'We have to be honest,' said Muharem Murselovic, persisting in not looking at Boris Danovic. 'You took part in all this.'

'Crimes happened, looting, killing,' Boris Danovic said.

'All that happens in war,' sighed Muharem Murselovic.

'The site has to be marked,' agreed Boris Danovic. 'Truth must not be concealed. We have to be ready for the memorial to be vandalised, but we have to persevere. It did happen in 1992. It will become a symbol of all the bad that happened so no one forgets.' Muharem Murselovic began to soften. 'This project is about memory of a place, and could become a successful method of reconciliation,' he said. 'It will encourage people to live and work together, a significant step forward in Prijedor. Personally I feel there should be more than one site marked in this way. I am not happy about the new bye-laws forbidding recognition of civilian suffering.' He was referring to the regulation passed recently at the Republika Srpska assembly stipulating that memorials be only for soldiers. 'There are memorials by the town hall for fallen fighters, also by the mine and by the school in Trnopolje.'

'If we continue this argument,' responded Boris Danovic defensively, 'I would have to insist that Serbs be allowed to put a plaque in Sarajevo. We need to mark all places of remembrance.'

'We are talking about Prijedor,' Muharem Murselovic said firmly.

We pointed out that our brief was specifically with Omarska.

Despite Muharem Murselovic and Boris Danovic holding their separate points of view and not engaging in a proper conversation, they drank wine and then left together. Muharem Murselovic was angry and this brief meeting did not allow for the expression of feelings. He clearly wanted to shake Boris Danovic and ask why he had gone along with the killing camp. At least they were prepared to sit together, but the weight of history crushed both of them. We respected both men's courage. They made speeches but did not know how to take the conversation further.

We hoped for more success with the women and prepared the first encounter between Serb and Bosniak women by gathering them in separate groups. First we met three women from the mine headquarters who seemed ready to talk.

All three had moved from suspicion about our motives, expecting us to criticize them, then through ambivalence about the project, warning us we would need the backing of the mayor, and finally to support and cooperation, as individuals rather than representatives of the mine. They understood the perils of the project, even the likelihood of failure which could backfire on them, but also the importance of this first step. They appreciated that we had not made unreasonable demands of them, and above all had listened to their views and valued their contribution. This commitment lasted up to and beyond the end of the project.

The mine women discussed the layout of the memorial, keeping it separate from the rest of the mine. One proposed a joint project of tree planting in memory of all victims of war on all sides, but not at Omarska.

Even talking to Serbs infuriated some of the Bosniak community, who were insisting that no Serb should be involved in the memorial project. Before bringing Emsuda Mujagic and Nusreta Sivac together with the mine women we had a confrontational meeting with Edin Ramulic and Seida Karabasic at the Izvor offices in Prijedor. After a brief summary of our progress, including suggestions about tree planting, Emsuda Mujagic wanting to turn the meadow around the white house into an 'oasis of peace', and our own proposals about an international competition to find a sculptor for the memorial, Edin Ramulic, again barely able to contain his fury, launched into a blistering attack:

'Your concept is flawed. Firstly, sculptures are unacceptable to Islam. Secondly, the place must be kept as it is. There were no trees there, and so none should be added. The fields are more important than the house. The media exaggerated the importance of the white house. People were interrogated, raped and murdered in all the management buildings. Horrendous things happened in the garage, also in the canteen and hangar. People were forced to drink oil, hung on hooks and made to bite each others testicles. At the red house no one survived, all were killed.' The red house was another shed-like building across the field from the white house. Edin Ramulic continued: 'The platform in front of the red house was a torture site. No building should be given priority. Going back to your idea about trees, had there been any, they might actually have helped prisoners escape. The trees you suggest would conceal the building, which is unacceptable. Thirdly there has been no consensus about a memorial at the white house. You have not yet met those people who are qualified and are the only ones who have a right to talk about this subject, those who survived and now live abroad. The white house should be fenced off and kept exactly as it is, adding nothing.'

Seida backed him: 'We talked to people from the diaspora who lost family members; and they are very upset at not being included in this process. Those who came last year on August 6th, to mark the day the camp was closed, everyone agreed with Edin that the whole complex of the mine must be honoured. People flooded into the administrative buildings, to the garage and the hangar, but not one went to the white house.'

It seemed as though both Seida Karabasic and Edin Ramulic were implying nothing especially important happened in this place, then Edin spat out: 'One of them suggested we throw a bucket of red paint over the white house to remind everyone that blood was spilt there. That would be a correct symbol of what happened!'

They accepted our proposal about the book with names of people who died there, but these should include those found in the mass grave at Kevljane. Edin Ramulic and Seida Karabasic insisted there must be a museum with computers and internet so people could give their opinions and comment on issues. 'All the buildings involved in the killing are not crucial to mine-production; administration can take place elsewhere. We want to give a warning: this must never happen again!'

Though they rejected our methods Edin Ramulic and Saida Karabasic wanted to be involved in the first meeting we were setting up later that week between as many people from all sides who wanted to discuss the memorial project, but Seida Karabasic suddenly decided she needed to be in Sarajevo and we feared that Edin Ramulic might disrupt the meeting at a time when we needed the temperate and cooperative voices on both sides to be heard, so Anel told him not to turn up.

The main purpose of bringing the mine women together with Emsuda Mujagic and Nusreta Sivac was to ensure a solid core of cooperation at the first 'concept' meeting. We intended this preparatory encounter to break the ice, initiate conversation and identify the important issues. Kemal Pervanic's brother Kasim had warned us that although Serbs, Croats and Bosniaks did business together, they never spoke about the war or what happened.

Emsuda Mujagic and Nusreta Sivac arrived first at the mine headquarters and we sat nervously waiting for the three management women in a large meeting room next to the manager's office. It became an issue that the mine people were mostly too busy to attend meetings, sometimes only one would turn up, or none at all. They always apologized politely. We asked for a representative who could liaise between us and the workers, but no one was prepared to take on a job which might label them as 'memorial-friendly'. However on this first crucial meeting all three women turned up. Serbs and Bosniaks faced each other across the wide table and smiled tentatively.

They introduced themselves formally, Nusreta Sivac, a former judge, taking charge, sitting forward in her chair and looking encouragingly at the other women. She explained her position as one of the initiators of the memorial project and member of the Association of Women of Bosnia and Herzegovina that included survivors. Immediately she apologized for the fracas on August 6th, only a month previously, when over a thousand Bosniaks turned up at the mine to mark the day of the camp's closure. Only two hundred had been expected. The crowds and cars created a parking problem, and interrupted the progress of a Serb wedding driving in the opposite direction. Insults were hurled, Serbs making a victory sign and telling the Bosniaks to go to hell. The visitors then overran the administrative buildings and some offices were broken into (it turned out that files were being searched to identify names of drivers and others involved in killings). Anel and others present had assured the mine management that apart from the office break-in the visit passed off reasonably peacefully considering the unexpected numbers. The visitors then heard of our project and were curious about developments. 'It was very unpleasant and could have got out of hand,' Nusreta Sivac explained. 'I informed the security guards about the damage.' The mine women did not complain, but nodded sympathetically. This was only to be expected, and clearly there had to be some kind of memorial in place as soon as possible to satisfy future visitors and returnees. They agreed on closing off the white house and its grounds from the rest of the mine, but allowing survivors in just two days of the year, on May 24th and August 6th, to visit and see all places where they were held and tortured. 'The noise of the machinery really upsets them,' Emsuda Mujagic said, 'reminding them painfully of what they suffered.' The mine women agreed the mine should be closed on those days but said nothing about relocating administration offices. They agreed about planting trees and that the memorial itself should be decided by survivors only.

The women talked politely for a while; then Kate Goslett, who until now had been observing and listening quietly at all our meetings, asked us to withdraw from the conversation, leaving the women and her together, just Emir Muhic, our translator, sitting nearby in case of need.

Suddenly the conversation became more animated, as Nusreta Sivac and Emsuda Mujagic told their stories and the mine women listened with tears in their eyes. Kate Goslett told us later how one of them talked about her Bosniak midwife and then suddenly in the middle of all the talk of horrors the women became animated about a mutual acquaintance: 'She's looking good for her age!' they gossiped and laughed loudly.

In contrast to Muharem Murselovic and Boris Danovic who could not look at each other while they delivered speeches, the women had frequent eye contact and were prepared to show emotion. Katerina Panic at the next meeting of the 'round table' widened her eyes in incredulity that either of these encounters had happened at all.

Whether these women established enough of a relationship to provide a firm core at the main meetings remained to be seen. Though they greeted each other subsequently with respect, a coolness and suspicion prevailed.

We needed to make sure Boris Danovic was present at the first 'concept' meeting, and knocked on his office door hoping he had not been discouraged by the conversation with Muharem

Murslovic. On the contrary he welcomed us warmly and seemed galvanized by our presence: 'If we concentrate too much on our past we cannot move forwards. We must avoid arguments about what happened. I know more about the history of 1989 because I was in a position to know. Crimes happened, regardless of how many, whether few or more. People know who happened to be there. We owe it to the dead and for the sake of the future to learn from our mistakes.' He had also been thinking about the memorial. 'The visitor's centre could be just behind or next to the white house. I designed the mine before the war, so I know the lay out. I went up with a sports pilot to get an aerial view.' He repeated his concern about the Dayton Agreement: 'It was the biggest mistake in the whole of Bosnia that they did not eliminate nationalist Serbs who are even now continuing the war.'

Croats had always been the smallest of the ethnic groups in this region, but after the war even this community had been decimated. Most fled to Croatia and never returned. The government welcomed them there and settled them in places where Serbs had been driven out. Since Croats had also been held and murdered at Omarska we had to find a representative to speak for them. The Catholic priest met us in a darkened office, seeming to fear even venturing out. His predecessor had been murdered on the streets, although people insisted it had not been an ethnically motivated crime, but a drunken attack that went out of control. We could not expect him to take part in the project, and Bishop Komarica had warned us not to ask. However Anel Alisic knew a feisty Croat woman who had refused to move to Croatia and insisted on staying in her home in Prijedor.

Mirjiana Verhabovic worked as a representative of Croat people and commissioner for returnees on the local council. 'I have worked here for forty years and am a communist,' she claimed proudly, pouring out glasses of home-made lemonade. Surprisingly, she felt scant respect for Bishop Komarica, reckoning that he had burnt himself out during the war and now had no energy for his flock. Being a communist she probably had been raised to be suspicious of religion, although holy pictures and crosses hung on the walls of her immaculate flat. The books and artefacts indicated a cultured life; she was one of the few educated people to survive the war and remained by choice in this 'black hole' of a town. She was the only Croat on the project.

At the end of the preparatory meeting between the women at the mine, Kate Goslett had asked them to describe their feelings in an image. Emsuda Mujagic spoke about sinking in a boat at sea, no help, but now the image was changing into a highway with many lanes. Mirjiana Verhabovic agreed with this image, but warned us to tread carefully and take account of Bosnian history, agreeing with Kate Goslett's observation: 'When men decide to go to war they forget to ask the women.'

Zarko Gvosden, the older Serb who attended the meeting at Hambarene, belonged to the same political party as Mirjiana Verhabovic, both committed communists. They wanted to be part of the project, representatives of the generation that knew Bosnia well before the war, and experienced the fighting and suffering on all sides. However Zarko Gvozden did not co-operate well with the phalanx of Serbs from the 'round table'. The young people were bored by his lectures, and he talked down to them patronizingly.

'The war started when I was thirty nine,' he told us. 'I asked myself why? I studied more history than ever before to find the answers about the ferocity of violence between neighbours. In Serb Orthodox history never before were women and children singled out to be killed as in my own town. Being Serb I belong to the side of the winners, but am unhappy about what we did. I want to separate the humane and intelligent people of all ethnic backgrounds from the inhumane and stupid ones.'

'I fear those,' said Mirjiana Verhabovic, 'there are too many of them around, and will try and spoil the project. Prijedor is the last black hole on the face of the earth. It will take lots of sanity to break the wings of these villains. The international community must help. On our own we cannot deal with such groups of extremes.'

THE BIG MEETINGS: ALL TOGETHER

The first meetings took place in the OSCE (Organization for Security and Cooperation in Europe) offices at Prijedor. Jeff Ford, head of office, allowed us the use of a large downstairs room where gradually all the people we had spoken with and invited sat in a circle and looked silently at each other; Boris Danovic and the women from the mine administration facing Muharem Murselovic, Azra Pasalic, Nusreta Sivac and Emsuda Mujagic while the young Serbs from the 'round table' sat between them. Everyone turned up.

Jeff Ford, along with the British Embassy representative at Banja Luka, the mine manager and Graham Day, Deputy High Representative and Head of Office in Banja Luka, formed our support and advisory group until all with the exception of Graham Day, tried to impose their pro-Serb perspective on the project. The mine manager needed to pacify the mayor and his cronies to protect the mine's interests; Jeff Ford and the British Embassy representative were afraid of upsetting Serb nationalist politicians. Their recommendation to employ a Serb to help with the administration, rather than our choice of a Bosniak, Anel Alisic, and a Serb Croat, Zoran Djukic, indicated a significant difference of approach. The Serb woman they had in mind was well-qualified, attractive with useful social skills, relaxed and charming with politicians. She would establish good relations with the mine and Serbs in places of influence, even Mayor Pavic perhaps, but not with the Bosniak community. A memorial being the main objective of this project, we had to negotiate the tricky currents of inter-ethnic relations in Prijedor with a team who could access all sides equally. Such advice from the international community did not inspire us with confidence. In fact our relations with the OSCE deteriorated when they suddenly and publicly withdrew their support for our process, not only jeopardizing the project but also our presence. That came after the third meeting.

But for now Jeff Ford gave a helpful introduction: 'These kinds of initiatives are crucial to any talks of reconciliation. The Soul of Europe is a catalyst.There is risk and courage for all who are attending this historic meeting, the first since the war, where different groups and ages are meeting to discuss painful and difficult issues. How do we remember those who died in Omarska? The purpose of this gathering is to create working groups to break the wall of silence. We are not friends but colleagues. We have to explore the difficult process of working on relationships with considerable differences. These can lead to arguments, but we need to work on this project despite our differences, acknowledging them, but continuing together. Former groups we set up in Banja Luka were not used to work with differences and so collapsed. I hope we can succeed.'

The young Serbs from the 'round table' then divided everyone into small groups. Jeff Ford took us to his office and explained the work of the OSCE on conflict prevention and human rights of minorities. In contrast to Jeff Ford's chumminess, telling us about his wife and child joining him in Prijedor and friendly suppers with the mine manager, his staff refused to look at us. Their hostility intensified with each meeting, blanking our greetings with a mocking grimace, keeping their eyes averted. Not even at the mine did we meet with such obvious antagonism. Did they consider our project to be a threat? Was something more sinister going on? Or had they been instructed to keep a distance?

While the OSCE staff for mysterious reasons turned their backs on us and muttered together in the kitchen area we looked out of the window at the groups talking below in the forecourt of the building and saw Nusreta Sivac and Emsuda Mujagic in intense conversation with Boris Danovic. Whatever else we managed to achieve we had provided these former victims and persecutor a space to confront each other, ask questions and try to find answers.

When the groups returned to the meeting room, Nusreta Sivac was the first to speak: 'Forty minutes we talked openly, candidly, personally and I have to say I am glad to have met the former mine manager. I heard of him but never knew him. In the post-war period I heard negative things about him. Now there are no misunderstandings. We agreed on everything we talked about, even on the most sensitive issues from the past and Omarska especially, while it was used as a killing camp. He knew what was going on but did not have a hand in it. We talked about issues of power and authority. He supports the project, agrees with it and will contribute to realize it.'

Emsuda Mujagic concurred: 'It was a pleasant meeting. The former mine manager tempered our unfounded prejudice against him.'

'I am glad we found common ground,' said Boris Danovic. 'It took a lot of effort to reach this. We have to mark the crimes for those who are still alive and for the future.'

Katerina Panic, the young journalist from the 'round table', had listened to their conversation and said: 'I was really impressed and surprised at the level of confidentiality, even though I myself had heard his name in negative contexts. I asked the women whether they trusted his candour. In fact it is now known Boris Danovic helped Bosniaks. We agreed that the memorial should not be small in scale, but as big as it needs to be.'

One of the mine management women had been in a group with Muharem Murselovic and also expressed relief at their encounter. She made a considerable leap forward: 'I think that we began the conversation positively, though we had never met before. It was friendly and honest. We all expressed our opinions. Mursel told us about the bad things that happened. When someone is able to talk about that it is always good. He was prepared to take part in our conversation, and we all agreed the place has to be marked. The proposed visitor's centre has to include the bad history, as well as stuff about the working of the mine, so everyone has a reason to visit. The future of our town depends on what we do.'

'I agree,' said Muharem Murselovic. 'We discussed everything in a friendly way. This method of marking the place is a good one. Bearing in mind that the mine's work must not be disrupted we have to reconcile work and the memorial. The mine is important for the economy, but we have to seek out ways of how to remember what happened. This is the first baby step.'

Sasha Drakulic, who had persuaded us to see Boris Danovic in the first place, seemed surprisingly content with this stage of the mediation process. Of all members of the 'round table', he prided himself on being the most sceptical and critical of our process. 'I can only add that it was great to hear at first hand from people who suffered and who are able to talk calmly about it. Mursel's heart beats faster at any mention of Omarska but there is no hate in him and he gave a good evaluation of this project; important because he is a leading politician.'

Zarko Gvozden, the older Serb, spoke at length about his group which consisted of Mirjiana Verhabovic, the only Croat present, and a number of young Serbs from the 'round table'. He reckoned that only he and Mirjiana Verhaboic understood the issues well enough to have an opinion, though he conceded that the 'younger men' were 'quite intelligent'. He added to what had already been agreed: 'The basic question is how the memorial can be made to reflect the intensity of suffering? We therefore disagree with having trees around the white house. The place should not be hidden from the eyes of visitors. There should be memorial plaques identifying the names of victims.'

Vedran, one of the first young Serbs to join the 'round table' and who then became the first to leave the project because he became adamant that only victims should be allowed to decide on a memorial and that Serbs had no right to be involved, looked deeply moved by the occasion and spoke: 'Of course we agree that the memorial is important. Only survivors and victims should be asked about it in the first place. No other solution is acceptable or moral. Consult them. Don't ignore them. They have to say what the memorial looks like. It should reflect the enormity of the crimes that happened here, the extent of suffering at the hands of soldiers, the media and politicians only because they were not Serbs. We have to emphasise the human tragedy and avoid politics.'

Mirjiana Verhabovic agreed with Zarko Gvozden: 'Don't hide the place, keep it revealed. Make the memorial educational as well as physical with literature and other material so future generations know the entire truth.'

Serbs, Bosniaks and the one Croat, young and old, agreed on three basic points: that the place needed to be marked, the mine's work should not be disrupted and the safety of visitors be taken into account. All agreed to continue this process.

The 'round table' gathered for lunch afterwards to discuss the meeting. 'We will achieve our aim,' said Tijana Glusac, a Serb student committed to the project enough to make the journey from Banja Luka to Prijedor for every meeting. 'It was important that opposites found a way of cooperating without negative tensions.'

Katerina Panic felt that the young Serbs should have introduced themselves and taken part rather than observing: 'Nusreta was the most famous survivor at the meeting,' she told us, 'and the former mine manager the most notorious name there.' Emsuda Mujagic had apparently broken the ice by telling him: 'I want to sit closer to you.'

Everyone asked for a media black out until the process had gone further and we began to discuss the idea of a conference which would host a presentation of the memorial agreed by all participants. Then the black out would be lifted. Also everyone needed to be fully informed and have access to all facts in booklet form, to counteract the climate of denial, hearsay and exaggerations on all sides.

Sasha Drakulic pointed out the sensitivity of our role: 'I am content to be part of the project but don't want to be publicly associated with the Soul of Europe.' He meant that this process of mediation had to be owned by the people themselves. The positive start however made him uneasy: 'I miss arguments. We are not there just to nod heads. I missed someone disagreeing. We need agreement at the end, but not at the beginning!'

To complete this stage of the process of mediation we visited all those present at this, the first of three 'concept' meetings, the concept referring to the project, not specifically the memorial, but a way of getting people to talk about the past together. We wanted to make sure all participants felt comfortable, so they would attend further meetings and take the process further.

The mine women expressed relief that people were prepared to discuss the memorial rationally, in other words were not aiming to close the mine down. Carrying on Emsuda Mujagic's image of a boat tossed in stormy waters, one of the mine women spoke of the boat now being steered down a river through dangerous currents. She also saw a spider web, but we could not be sure whether this represented a network of different ideas or a trap. Another mine woman expressed relief that though opinions varied, everyone reached a shared conclusion to mark the place. 'We knew we would not agree, but we will work on the project.' The mine woman's image of a boat being steered through dangerous currents accurately forecast the later stages of the project when extreme opinions from both sides would move invisibly under the surface, threatening to capsize us all.

Two important figures, a Bosniak and a Serb, began to emerge as significant figures in the project. Whatever success we achieved would be down to these influential leaders of the community.

First of these was Azra Pasalic who had been from the beginning a committed supporter of the process, and we needed her shrewd political skills as Speaker of the Municipal Assembly and someone constantly in touch with Mayor Pavic to help guide the project. 'Our positions make us equal, the mayor and I,' she told us. 'But he does not treat me as an equal. He makes plans but does not bother to consult me. So now I phone him informally. He prefers that. I treat him as a friend.'

Then there was the director of the mine who needed time to trust us. As the process continued he took considerable risks supporting us. At our first meetings we feared his cautious response. His change of heart apart from being touching, indicated the strengthening of the project and became a vindication of a painstaking process of giving confidence to people from both sides to take the first painful steps towards dialogue, cooperation and maybe eventually to reconciliation. Azra Pasalic provided a check on the mayor and also held the disparate strands of the Bosniak community together at crucial stages of the project. The mine director bravely took responsibility for bringing the mine and its staff alongside. The future of his community mattered to him, and he understood the wider perspective of such a process, which would ensure the well-being and functioning of the mine not just for the short term but for generations. For the director the mine was home. His office was comfortable, filled with paintings, icons and artefacts, maps and photographs of the mine, a desk piled high with documents. Saint Sava and Saint Varvara, patron saint of miners, watched over his desk.

Azra Pasalic and the mine director helped steer this difficult project. When we met with obstacles that impeded progress these two understood the long term needs of their community regarding the memorial and both would hold the vision.

The mine director could not come to the first meeting, but his wife, a doctor and also a politician, a member of Milorad Dodik's party, attended. She and Azra Pasalic happened to be friends and colleagues. When Azra took up her position as Speaker of the Assembly, a Bosniak as stipulated by the international community in case of a Serb mayor (in the Bosnian Federation where mayors tended to be Bosniak, then the speakers would have to be Serb) and she faced the hostile ranks of mostly Serb delegates and representatives from all over the municipality, the mine director's wife made a point of crossing the floor and publicly welcoming her.

'Now the memorial is getting closer my feelings are changing: I can see it happening,' said Azra Pasalic at our follow up conversation with her and the mine director's wife after the first concept meeting. 'Memorial centres must be places which prevent atrocities ever happening again.' She understood the difference between memorials to fallen soldiers and those that marked crimes.

Azra's son had been a fourteen year old refugee in the United States. She monitored his development there as a student from afar. He and fellow students were taken to the Holocaust museum in New York. 'My son went pale. He asked one of the teachers what it was all about. The teacher knew he came from Bosnia. Now my son has a successful career in information technology. His heart is determined not to repeat the mistakes of the past. The museum visit helped purge bad thoughts that were tormenting him, anger and desire for revenge. Now he talks about returning to Bosnia, creating a visitors centre for children to learn what happened. Omarska needs marking to honour the sacrifices and suffering of victims, to understand remorse and sorrow, to learn from it. We cannot wait. This is the moment. We have to learn from history now while people are still around who survived, so no one can dispute or contest what happened.'

'Remember the turbulent history of this region,' remarked the mine director's wife, having agreed with the proposals for a memorial to honour the victims, but insisting that it should be dignified and 'calming'. 'There are memorials to victims of fascism at Kozara, but they were not sufficient to prevent the next war. It will happen again if we are not careful. All my political work is preventative. I want my children to learn from the past.'

They remembered the mine always being a central part of the region's economy, and how it raised beautiful buildings in Prijedor. 'The mine always brought prosperity to Prijedor. I want to make the mine owners richer if we succeed in this project,' said Azra Pasalic, hopeful of their generosity. The mine director's wife added: 'As a citizen of Prijedor I will insist that profits be redirected to good projects and social issues. The money should not be squandered.'

'Silence is an accomplice to crimes,' said Azra Pasalic, commenting positively on the mayor's presence at the mass funeral in July. 'We appreciated his presence. He faced criticism. Only when we all sit down and talk together can we reach a resolution. Perpetrators must also take part and find a compromise. We need to identify obstacles and tackle them and always look for the good sides in human beings. But the mayor is an elusive man. You will need to work on him more. Maybe you should play tennis with him! Teach him how to be a team player!'

Meetings with Azra Pasalic were always cheerful occasions. Her room was airier and lighter than anywhere else in the town hall. Azra always offered fruit as well as drinks, peeling and slicing apples for guests, and at her house-cum-surgery where the 'round table' met she cut up large melons on particularly hot days and served them to the young people who were discussing the project in the shade of a large walnut tree. Azra was deeply touched by the young Serbs and Bosniaks wrestling with issues that had scarred their lives and prospects, trying to make a better future out of a present that seemed hopeless.

We spoke with the mine director about tying the memorial in with a visitor's centre at the mine. Such centres in mines all over the world helped explain the workings of what might seem a mysterious and forbiddingly complex process, digging vast craters and despoiling the environment. Considering the importance of the mine to the region's economy, a visitor's centre would improve public relations between the mine and Prijedor. It needed to tell the whole history of the mine going back to Ancient Roman times up to the present including its use as a killing camp. The museum educated future generations about the science of mining and provided a warning so that such misuse and atrocities never happened again.

'You are our best PR,' the mine director enthused after shaking our hands warmly and pressing our arms, 'because you have done your best to understand our country, our people and our problems. You send a message to visitors and those who live and work here, different from the usual negative information. You must see this mission through and we have all to make sure the results endure; to work together towards such a resolution. Having all these discussions with so many different people and institutions is worthwhile. We can't do it ourselves, although we should have done it. We appreciate you helping us. As you can see we have been too busy with other activities, but now we have you. I am certain we will achieve our objective. You have many ideas about the future and we need to listen to you. Your knowledge and experience of different peoples gave birth to this concept. Perhaps I have different ideas. But I probably wouldn't have the time to achieve them. You create breadth by dealing in a wider perspective. You extended the picture from a narrow to a broader concept. Independently from the white house, whatever form that takes, your proposal for a visitor's centre is rich and profound. Its content will reflect all activities of the mine and its history. These will improve quality of life and provide hope for all who live and work here. The future is what we need to care about. People will see that in the centre. In the next days we are discussing plans for the mine in the next twenty years, and we will incorporate your new ideas. The mine works on a smaller scale than before, although we are opening new seams, but is still the biggest organization in the municipality. You are contributing significantly to these discussions. I now have a picture of the future which I did not see before.'

In the evening we drank wine and had supper at La Pont with the mine director and his wife. We talked about their childhood and courtship in Bosanska Krupa, now in the Bosnia Federation, of art and the unique beauty of the Bosnian countryside.

KILLING THE LIGHT

We took a calculated risk showing Rezak Hukanovic's film about the killing camp at Omarska to the young Serbs from the 'round table' as well as a group of Serb displaced people, who felt that their suffering in the war had gone unnoticed by the international community. So far people had talked about their experiences and confronted each other with personal opinions. Now everyone would watch one person's particular story. The film made concrete and inescapable what up to now might have seemed unreal to those who had not been through the trauma. The film did not flinch from telling everything as it was.

On film Rezak speaks calmly and emotionlessly to camera about his incarceration and torture in Omarska, specifically the white house, and describes what happened to friends and colleagues who did not survive. In the background the faces of his wife and son express the torment he either cannot or refuses to show, and it is their sorrow beyond tears, frozen anger and pain of memory that underline the brutal facts. The film was made in Sweden before his return to Prijedor. Wife and son remained there.

At a preview of the film in Azra Pasalic's house, before showing it to the group, we were shocked at the reminder of the savagery of what happened, medieval in its ferocity. No one talked about this aspect of the war. A detailed history, from all sides, about what happened a little over a decade ago in Bosnia still needed to be written. It took ten years after the Second World War for the first documentary to be shown about Auschwitz. *Night and Fog*, a forty minute documentary (1955, but not widely shown in Germany until the 1960's) by the French director Alain Resnais shocked a young generation who knew little or nothing of the truth about concentration camps, to such an extent that Germany in particularly was disrupted by youth riots and student revolts leading to the Red Army Faction and urban terrorism. It took almost fifty years after the Second World War for a full scale documentary to do justice to the Holocaust, *Shoah* by Claude Lanzmann (another French director). People were now seeing Rezak Hukanovic's *Killing the Light* thirteen years after the event. The Republika Srpska refused to show it on television for fear of traumatising viewers. 'It is too soon!' they claimed. But as Azra Pasalic pointed out, it cannot be soon enough, because the longer the truth is suppressed, the worse the consequences for the next generations.

For the first time I felt unable to enter a discussion after seeing the film. Luckily Anel and Zoran had fixed for me to play the piano at Prijedor's music school. The director, dressed in a threadbare suit and whom I mistook for the porter, lead me to an airy room with a grand piano and shut the door so I could be alone and undisturbed. Playing through Bach's *Art of the Fugue*, with its tranquil and densely contrapuntal beauty, I attempted to find some kind of equilibrium.

The 'round table' meanwhile discussed how such a film could be presented and viewed. We did not aim to inflame but to educate. This told one harrowing story among thousands, including those of the Serb displaced people who also suffered persecution, death and loss. The group watching the film needed to be prepared, not to spare their feelings, but to prevent them resisting the truth it spoke. Everyone suffered in the war, some more than others. This story gave an account of some of the worst atrocities to take place. All people seeing the film needed to recognize their common humanity.

The 'round table' suggested we invite teenagers from Prijedor to the showing. Anel introduced us to a group of them from Info Point, an organization funded by the municipality which acted as an umbrella for various youth community projects such as sports and culture. These young people were not afraid to talk about the past. When asked about the priorities for their lives they gave an unexpected response. Given the high unemployment rate in Prijedor and lack of opportunities, we expected jobs to be top of their agenda. They told us that truth was more important. 'We need to know what happened. It is impossible to lead normal lives given the history of this place. We have to find a sign of hope. The world knows what went on here. Our media tells us lies and we have to be told the truth. I don't know it. You don't know it. The truth has to come first, otherwise we have no future.'

They raised the issue of who writes history. History is the story of people's lives, their parents, their grandparents, regardless of race or background. Che Guevara on being charged with being responsible for starting violent revolution responded: 'We were accused of going into the villages, burning the houses and killing people. Not so. We gathered the people together and invited them to tell the story of their lives. That was the revolution.'

Some of the teenagers at Info Point had just taken part in a satirical play directed by an English theatre workshop, Wolf and Water.The sketches fearlessly lampooned corrupt politicians and municipality workers, culminating in a finale which showed officials drawing a line on the floor of a lift to separate Bosniaks and Serbs. People kept arriving to enter the lift and eventually lost patience with the officials, pushing them out of the way and everyone crushed in together. Audiences in both Bosniak Kozarac and Serb Prijedor cheered loudly, especially at the punch line when someone in the crowded lift farted. Satire and farce made a potent mixture.

Given the lack of truth and the prevalence of contested history in the whole of Bosnia the young people of Info Point proposed creating a theatre piece that would cover a period of history from the point of view of each ethnic group and also suggested a project for collecting stories, anonymously, from across the region. The theatre piece would be funny and serious. 'It will be important for the future of Bosnia and for the truth to be told,' they said.

This conversation persuaded us that they should be invited to see Rezak Hukanovic's *Killing the Light*.

Rezak Hukanovic hesitated to introduce the film, and he almost didn't turn up, but his presence helped the audience absorb the shocking truth. If they did not want to respond they could leave in silence, as I had done after the preview. Rezak being there had a calming effect, especially on the teenagers who were lost for words. The Serb survivors, who complained that their stories had not been told, looked at him and were moved to tears. His story did not preclude theirs.

Mirsad Duratovic from Hambarene also came to see the film. As it proceeded, he began to shake and cry. He and Rezak Hukanovic had been through the same experience, Mirsad as a seventeen year old boy.

In private conversation with Mirsad Duratovic afterwards we commented on his normally calm and positive demeanour, how well he seemed to have survived these horrors. He stroked his skin meaningfully and said: 'Underneath is different. You know that I have not been able to share the same bed with my wife for years. I keep waking up, hitting out, shouting. On August 6th I took my seven year old son to Omarska. He should know what happened there.'

The elderly displaced Serbs looked defeated by the film and by their situation. We had seen many like them in our years travelling throughout Bosnia. We observed them forming long queues in Belgrade waiting for help, and in the Republika Srpska being offered homes once occupied by Bosniaks then having to move on, never able to settle, confused and bitter, not knowing who to blame and also feeling guilty for being responsible for their fate.

Djordje Jez, their leader, a former Serb soldier from Bosanska Krupa, could barely suppress his fury at being forced to watch Rezak Hukanovic's film, although he had been told about it. He explained to us later that now only Bosniaks received sympathy, and no one cared about displaced Serbs. 'The film should not have been played. You should have shown something less upsetting to the survivors. It is too soon for such films. Time has to heal. I fought in the war. On September 16th in 1992 I was badly injured and the last ambulance took me away from Bosanska Krupa. We met columns of people fleeing. My wife and children stayed then managed to get military transport out of town. I was not able to take even a spoon from my home, which my father owned and built up. You speak about a memorial at the mine. Don't rush this project.'

The day after showing the film a bomb exploded outside Rezak Hukanovic's house.

This brought home to the younger members of the audience, the 'round table' and the teenagers from Info Point that the war between the communities had not ended. They decided to visit Omarska and also Sejkovac and see for themselves the places where Bosniaks were tortured and killed, and the bodies of those found in mass graves were still waiting to be identified.

The mayor, hearing about our group meetings, needed to keep his blue eyes on us. When we next saw him, after repeating speeches about the importance of international investment and the mine he gave us a warning: 'To be honest, what you are doing is a burden to me. I don't like to have anything to do with this project. I don't see any progress. You are moving too quickly. Over time these things will fade away and be forgotten. Rushing and forcing decisions will not succeed.'

He did not attend a meeting as promised between his cabinet and participants of the project. Biljiana Malbasic, his head of finances, represented him. She had earlier refused our invitation to visit Sejkovac with other members of the cabinet. She attacked the project and saw no purpose in any memorial at the mine. Reminders of the past in her opinion would increase bad feeling in the community.

'We don't need your help!' she concluded, hoping to shut the door on us finally.

Muharem Murselovic responded by telling his story, seventy three days incarcerated at the mine, adding: 'People need to know what happened. I know the attitudes of people towards Omarska. People still claim nothing happened. That is the point of the entire story and I myself living here since after the war. The fact is we all have to square up to what happened. The memorial will remind people that it should never happen again. Victims are the ones to be consulted about details. Radical opinions should be reconciled. Some people think the mine should be closed down – remember that is a fact. This is a place where hundreds were murdered. There should be nothing here but a memorial. That is a radical opinion and many people agree with it. Myself I think we should look for a middle ground. The mine is a lynchpin of the region, its main employer, and it has to prosper and work. Therefore we need to find a balance as to how we mark the place. Both ends should be met. We have to reach a compromise. Consult victims and survivors. It is a sacred place. Over two thousand visited on August 6th. Next year there will be six thousand or more. The international community were surprised at the numbers, survivors even bringing babies in prams. They wanted to show their children. So a middle ground has to be found, a reconciliation of extremes.'

Biljana Malbasic folded her arms across her breast, triumphant in the knowledge she spoke for the mayor: 'I have no response for Mr Murselovic. We have been talking for over five years and never reached agreement. Mr Murselovic mistrusts everybody. Of course we all know what happened. I say we need to forget. I respect his efforts to fight for his personal rights and his people but I cannot condone his attitude that he only cares for what happened in Prijedor and no where else in Bosnia. Criminals have been sent to The Hague, indicted and punished, so nothing more needs be done. I will never allow anyone to force me to feel shame for being a Serb.In fact I am offended because I am forced to feel shame for something I am not guilty of. Omarskas happened everywhere!'

The rest of the cabinet agreed with her (the only Bosniak, Mirsad Islamovic, being fortunately absent, as he would have been upset by this tirade) and some went further claiming the extreme Bosniak party in the Federation, the SDA, interfered in the judicial process and there were many Bosniak criminals not indicted yet.

We explained that the process of mediation meant people had to talk together like this, hear and try to understand each other and that our brief only covered Omarska. Bosnia was like everywhere else, we are all human beings trying to live at peace with each other. Biljana Malbasic seized on this observation that was not meant to be flippant: 'Bosnia is not like anywhere else,' she declared forcefully. 'Bosnia has a different history to anyone. Bosnia is different!' She sat back in her chair, arms folded again and eyes triumphant at having won the argument. From that moment she would have nothing more to do with the project and refused to meet us again. Muharem Murselovic was so upset that he took us back to his office and lectured us for an hour, repeating all he had told us before, his voice building to a high-pitched scream. After witnessing his encounter with the mayor's cabinet we understood why he tended to shout so much, even when speaking to us privately: they paid him no attention, no one heard him.

WHITE WATERS AND FAULT LINES
A picture on my hotel room depicted two figures on a raft negotiating the foaming waters of the River Vrbas as it cuts through a deep gorge on its way to Banja Luka. We now found ourselves in the middle of such rapids.

Reports of our confrontations with the mayor's cabinet reached Jeff Ford at the Organization for Security and Cooperation in Europe (OSCE) office in Prijedor. This accounted for a sudden withdrawal of his support for the project. Without warning us Jeff Ford announced this change of policy at the next group meeting.

Azra Pasalic and Vesna Jelaca, the mine women, Emsuda Mujagic and Nusreta Sivac were unable to conceal their dismay, all fixing us with a pitying gaze as Jeff Ford delivered his speech. The men lowered their eyes and seethed. When Emir, our interpreter, began to translate as usual, Jeff Ford stopped him brusquely, saying he preferred his own translator. This rude put-down gave a hint of what was to follow.

'The OSCE along with the Office of the High Representative are here only in an advisory capacity. We give no direction and do not control. There is no predetermined outcome. The Soul of Europe are independent mediators,' he began before delivering the first body blow which stunned everyone there and made us realize the vulnerability of our position. 'We do not endorse their views,' he declared emphatically. 'We are a neutral party. We may have personal opinions but we have no views about memorial centres in Omarska. You may continue your discussion now. We needed to make that clear.'

The rug had been pulled from under our feet. The sympathetic looks directed at us from all the women, Serb and Bosniak, now sitting next to each other in the circle, indicated solid support for us and the project. We broke the subsequent shocked silence by pretending we had heard differently, thanked Jeff Ford for offering us this space and spoke briefly about mediation, hoping a variety of concepts for the memorial would emerge from many conversations. We encouraged the participants to talk about what happened from a personal perspective, not as representatives of organizations. Then as quickly as possible we left the 'round table' to divide the participants into groups. Jeff Ford took us upstairs. Not even the mayor at his most menacing alarmed us more. The people downstairs were a priority, so we avoided immediate confrontation with the man we had assumed to be our ally. We remembered how he and his staff had already put us in danger by setting up meetings with extreme nationalists who now knew our identities and could eliminate us as they pleased. Jeff Ford had claimed these people to be moderates, even though their criminal connections and political affiliations made it obvious they would be hostile to the project. Graham Day from the Office of the High Representative afterwards assured us it had been a mistake on Jeff Ford's part, a clumsy attempt to distance his organization from being seen in any way to be partial to Bosniaks and memorials, but our experiences now told us that the OSCE seemed to be trying to scupper our project.

'He did us a favour,' Anel commented later dismissing our

anxieties about possible consequences for us and the project. 'People are suspicious of these international organizations and accuse them of earning good money on the back of Bosnia's suffering. Now you are seen to be independent of influence and people will actually respect you more. This will only be good for the project. We don't need to meet in the OSCE offices. There are other places more neutral.'

However, Muharem Murselovic delivered a blistering attack on the OSCE at the National Assembly in Banja Luka. Far from seeming to be impartial, the organization was seen to be pro-Serb.

'Nervous Nellies!' snorted Graham Day. 'They just don't like to rock the boat, but you can't do this kind of mediation work without ruffling feathers and breaking crockery.'

However he recognized a more serious consequence of this faux pas from Jeff Ford. The two of us Graham Day considered to be safe, but Anel, Zoran and other young Serbs who had put themselves on the line for the project were now in danger. All of them had already been threatened. 'Who are these young Serbs?' the mayor had demanded to know, and stopped funding their organization Info Point, further making its life difficult by cutting off utilities and heat in the winter. The young people showed no anxiety and persisted in their support for the project. With respect for their safety we consulted Anel and Zoran at every step but reserving the final decisions for ourselves.

Graham Day confirmed our fear that the rest of the international community did not support us: 'too much risk, too little gain.' It deemed our process to be too touchy-feely and the results too intangible and open-ended. Politicians preferred more obviously robust methods, though Graham Day knew that our process of getting people from both sides to sit and talk together was far from 'soft'. Therefore our centre of gravity for reflection and support had to come from the people we worked with, the 'round table' especially.

The meeting at the OSCE offices became a turning point in the project. Participants now needed to build up a momentum which would push the memorial to completion. Serb politicians and representatives from the mayor's cabinet, who came to see what was being said, did not attend further meetings, and withdrew along with the OSCE. The rest of the participants remained resolute. These included a young Serb politician from Milorad Dodik's party, Nino Jauz, who bravely declared his unqualified support. However the solid agreement and high hopes of the first months of the project now fractured in arguments over procedures and how the project should continue. A few dropped out of the process, including Vedran the philosopher and Sasha Drakulic. Vedran and Sasha supported the memorial, but they disagreed with the process. Passionate arguments tended to disrupt meetings at a time when the group needed to display unanimity. These fractures became a significant feature of the third phase of the mediation process, meetings specifically to discuss the memorial and prepare for a conference where an agreed concept for the memorial would be presented.

The group meeting at the OSCE included officials from the mayor's cabinet, for whom Jeff Ford's statement came as a relief, and possibly it had been meant for them to hear and report back to the mayor. They also heard in alarm the participants deciding to start discussion of the memorial at future groups.

'The memorial at Omarska has to be a house of no words,' declared Mirsad Islamovic, the one Bosniak member of the mayor's cabinet, and speaking for his group which included Serb politicians. As a representative of the Bosniak nationalist party, the SDA, he later became more sceptical of our mediation methods, saying we gave too much attention to Serbs. For now he approved. 'I was not happy with my group, but at least we agreed on one thing. Crimes were committed and therefore the place deserves a memorial where people can go and remember and pay their respects to those who died. It should express sorrow and remorse. Everyone needs a place of silence. We like the idea of footpaths leading indirectly to the white house.' He then made disparaging remarks about the new owners of the mine: 'No Bosniaks were present at the negotiations concerning the sale of the mine. Our group disagreed about a visitors centre. But we can discuss this matter in the future.'

Muharem Murselovic summed up the decisions of his group which included the secretary of the mayor's cabinet and women from the mine headquarters: 'I rarely speak for a group, usually my opinions are my own,' he began. 'It was good to talk. We had a divergence of opinion on technical details. We discussed first who should decide. We do not represent anyone. It seems the new management want to see the place marked. As people we can only give our own views, but we also create public opinion and an atmosphere that will help overcome the past so it doesn't happen again. At first I agreed with everything said, which surprised me because I did not expect that. We have to mark the place, but we must not disrupt the working of the mine. This is physically possible. As to questioning the facts, I was there. I understand the intensity of the horrors that took place. About six hundred people work there now. There is a chance of growth. We need to reconcile oppositions. We agreed it's possible. I have to say finally that I feared the discussion would go in the wrong direction. None of us support grandiose monuments. The white house is enough. It can be fenced off and we will work towards a solution of what to do with the building, but that is premature.'

Dusan Tubin, the secretary of the mayor's cabinet agreed that the place had to be marked but gave warning that any decision needed authorization from the municipality. 'If the new mine owners do this without consent, then why am I part of the decision process?' he said disingenuously, knowing that without the mayor's permission there would be no memorial and no project: 'Every decision has to go through the local council and must be approved.'

Azra Pasalic interrupted by suggesting the white house could be fenced off.

The location of the white house became a bone of contention after the conference: who owned the land, the mine or the local authorities? Muharem Murselovic, thinking to avoid unnecessary conflict with the authorities over new buildings or changed use of land, announced firmly: 'There is no need to build anything new.

It exists now as it is and will exist in the future.'

One of the mine women in the group changed the subject, saying encouragingly: 'Murselovic pointed out the most important issue: we need to develop positive public attitudes. This will help our children in the future to live together.'

Her father had been director of the mine before the war. She arranged for us to meet with him at the La Pont restaurant earlier on our visit in June. This distinguished looking man, tall, slim and handsome like his daughter, held privileged posts under the communist regime of the former Yugoslavia and now spent his retirement tending orchards in the hills outside Prijedor. He told us he had ordered the white house built to shelter miners from the rain, and spoke bitterly about its subsequent use as a place of murder and torture. 'I would never have had it built had I known that would happen there!' he exclaimed, then proceeded to lecture us on the history of Yugoslavia, the impossibility of different ethnic groups living together. He had transported Bosniak women and children to Trnopolje, claiming it to be a transit camp from which they would be taken abroad, and remained convinced that he had done them a favour. As to the mine employing Bosniaks again he warned us: 'Bosniaks can expect to be murdered and thrown down the mine for crimes that were done against Serbs.' His daughter had a more positive attitude to different communities living and working together.

As did Niki, a young Serb artist and rock singer from the 'round table', who had been nominated to report on the conclusions of the third group. One of the few young Serbs we met who had married, he brought his new-born baby to a group meeting. We paid special attention to the tiny visitor and explained: 'We are doing this project for his future!' At a later private meeting Niki unburdened his history to us. His brother in law had taken part in a notorious massacre of Bosniaks on Mount Vlasic. The victims had been taken to a high rock face, shot in the back of the head and pushed over. The brother-in-law was one of the few criminals who gave themselves up when war ended. In prison now after a trial at The Hague, for years he remained a hero to the Serb community at large, but public attitudes were changing. 'He brought shame on our family,' said Niki, more in sadness than anger. 'My family did something bad. I want to do something good.' But his father worried about Niki's involvement in the project. The father believed that loyalty to Serb nationalism still counted, and feared for the safety of his son being considered a traitor. 'I am not afraid,' said Niki. 'He may be my father but I can have my own opinions.' It touched me that on finding out it was my birthday he gave me a video of the Bosnian Oscar-winning film, *No Man's Land*, an acute tragi-comic examination of the Bosnian condition, a place where ethnic communities tear themselves apart and the international community looks on with a mixture of self-interest, helplessness and cynicism. The film ends with the image of a man lying on an unexploded mine, abandoned by two companions, one provoked into killing the other, and a film-crew, turning their back on him as he waits for his own death.

'We came to three conclusions,' Niki reported from his group at the meeting in the OSCE room. 'Firstly, the memorial centre or whatever is decided has to be private and fenced off so visitors don't have to be protected while they reach the site. Secondly, we concluded that we must take advantage of the new mine owners' intentions, even though we question their motives. I personally don't consider that morality, candour or sincerity on their part have anything to do with the memorial. They want to profit from the suffering of people and the evil that was done here. Nor are they interested in a spirit of coexistence between peoples. They see the memorial as propaganda for themselves. But we don't want to dispute crimes, so our third conclusion concerns the memorial: it needs to be done in a dignified way and people must be free to visit at all times and have a sense of what suffering happened there so it never happens again.'

We noted the positive energy in the group, despite the shock announcement of the OSCE withdrawing its support for the memorial, which had the effect of galvanizing all the people to focus on the memorial. Careful preparation, nurturing the 'yeast' of the 'round table' and encouraging individuals from all ethnic backgrounds to take the project forward was already helping the participants resist destabilization of the process from any quarter.

This new strength in the group proved itself in a vigorous discussion where all sides shared their opinions. Dusan Tubin, the secretary of the mayor's cabinet who had sat throughout the meeting looking bored and staring out of the window, insisted that only the mayor should decide about a memorial, and not the people present whom he considered unqualified, being neither the mine owners nor leading politicians. Mirsad Islamovic, the Bosniak SDA representative in the cabinet ignored this view along with the other participants, saying to us: 'Thank you for listening to our opinions. The new mine owners are in a position do what they please. But you understand us well, and what we want. Remember we are talking about over a thousand missing and murdered people. I was in the same group as Mr Danovic and asked about his role in the mine in 1992, why he had not voiced his disapproval. Hopefully we reach a solution that pleases everybody, nothing grandiose, as Murselovic said, but something serious to mark the place.'

Boris Danovic agreed it had been a difficult encounter in his group: 'There were accusations made without facts, and things got a bit whipped up. But I will continue.' It turned out that Azra Pasalic gave Mirsad Islamovic a dressing down in the group session for attacking Boris Danovic, telling him: 'This man is prepared to sit with you in the same room, face to face, to talk and support the project, in spite of what he did. Be civil to him!' Boris Danovic continued by promising to show everyone round the mine and find the best place for the memorial. Most of the participants appreciated his presence, but Mirsad Islamovic did not attend anymore meetings, belonging to that group of survivors who resisted any involvement by Serbs, especially someone they considered a criminal.

One of the women from the mine management reminded everyone that the project was about good community relations: 'When the project works it will benefit the mine owners. We have to trust their honesty and sincerity that the memorial is not just a piece of propaganda. No promotion should be made.'

'I am pleasantly surprised by the mine management,' said Muharem Murselovic. Then he reacted to Jeff Ford's remarks at the beginning of the meeting: 'I am disappointed by his statement.' Later he would attack the OSCE at the National Assembly. For now he concentrated on the meeting: 'I was not in the group with Mirsad Islamovic, who spoke nonsense apparently. But the mine management grasps the importance of the whole issue. They know what it means to be unemployed, and have steady jobs now. Any threat to the security of the mine is a sword of Damocles hanging over them if nothing is done about the memorial. But in defence of Mirsad Islamovic I have to say these radical opinions arise from the extent of the evil that happened here. People still believe silence achieves something. It is we who must make the decision. People don't want to take responsibility or have anything to do with the matter. They play a waiting game, just hoping for change. The international community will withdraw one day, and perhaps they should leave now. Then let's see what happens!' He was making the assumption that the ethnic cleansing and fighting would continue.

Mirjana Verhabovic, the only Croat participant, had a more cynical interpretation of our process: 'It seems our involvement is just for social purposes, window-dressing, and not for any practical results. People keep telling us that we need permission from the mayor, who represents the opinion of all Serbs. But he is our main obstacle.'

Muharem Murselovic took advantage of this opportunity to address a mixed audience, including the OSCE, saying: 'The international community closed the camps and turned their backs, leaving victims' bodies being moved around to different mass graves, permitting the Serbs to complete the job.'

He saw himself representing all Bosniaks in his country, being their politician and orator who told the truth as it was and able to express the despair, demands and hopes of his community. He continued: 'Today we face many problems as a result of the international community's actions. The general feeling in Prijedor is that the dust of denial covers the facts. I lived here all my life and am familiar with the views of the Serb majority. Serbs know the truth: they planned something monstrous and executed their plan. Three and a half thousand were murdered in the town. The cream of Prijedor's citizenry was displaced and liquidated. Here we still are, in a country where the relative majority used to be Bosniak. But in 1995 the international community agreed to the creation of the Republika Srpska. What kind of country is this where I returned? We want to be treated as equals and be allowed to mark our places of suffering. Serbs say we are impertinent and we constantly give in to them. The Republika Srpska constitution is hollow; no one follows it, or the amendments. Serbs openly declare open government to be not applicable here. They even pass laws saying that civil war victims should not be allowed memorials, so not recognizing a single non-Serb victim. A woman has photographs of her six sons all murdered in front of their house, but she cannot get them recognized as victims of war because she was late in reporting the murders and did not have any medical evidence, the bodies disappeared. There are no words for such injustice. There is even a new law declaring all civilian victims to be only Serb, ignoring the numbers of exhumed bodies of murdered Bosniaks. We lived here and survived for five hundred years. It is our home, but people wanted to eradicate us.'

Mirjana Verhabovic felt inspired by this outburst to speak for her Croat community: 'Croats fled from Bosnia back to Croatia and were settled in villages and homes that belonged to Serbs. The state subsidized them with homes and cattle, so Croats have no intention of returning to Bosnia. But I and a priest friend who was held in Omarska did return. Now after thirteen years it is futile to talk of returning. Bishop Komarica did nothing about it. Local priests have no influence anyway. All Croats will vanish from this area in the fullness of time. They have better lives in Croatia. But Bosniaks had no choice, this always was their home and they have nowhere else to go. So they have to fight for survival here. Soon only cemeteries will show that once Croats lived here. The international community propagates a devious lie about returnees. When the war ended everyone was encouraged to return to Prijedor. The naïve ones like me did so, only to be attacked from all sides, including Bosniaks. I was criticised for wanting my property back, but I felt everyone should be doing that. I started the process. We were welcomed with protests and bombs that blew up our homes. The international community allowed this to happen, and their timidity even encouraged it. After eight years here I am now considering leaving Prijedor. There is no change in the Republika Srpska. There is no future for Croats or Bosniaks here.'

At this point the meeting broke up, the participants with the exception of the mayor's cabinet agreeing to meet the following month in smaller groups to discuss the memorial in more detail and prepare a presentation for the conference.

Three responses summed up the state of the process and the project, all participants aware of the enormity of the task, recognizing the rifts between the communities which at least people were beginning to talk about together.

First Serb Zoran, our project manager, vented his feelings. His despair made him even more determined to bring the project to a positive conclusion.

'After this meeting I have to ask myself: how can I carry on living in Bosnia?' he said. 'Why? I came aboard this project as a human being, to deal with the problems from the point of view of humanity, not for political or ethnic reasons. I don't want ideologies and politicians deciding what we should do. We don't share the same opinions, Serbs and Bosniaks, but we all went through suffering, all three sides caused suffering. I respect the suffering of Murselovic who is a key person in our project, but I disagree with his political views. I agree with facts. When he talks about the Civil Victims Law, you have to bear in mind the same situation exists in the Federation. A friend of mine, Violetta from Bugojno in the Federation, had her whole family slaughtered by Bosniaks. Now she lives in Prijedor because she has no rights in the Federation. She cannot even get her property back. That happened to a large number of Serb returnees there. The same things happen on all sides. Our politicians should get rid of this law in both entities, adjust it, unify. Until they behave positively on this issue there will never be unity in the BiH and nothing will improve. I sense hatred of a nation on all sides. This must not happen in our project. The suffering of the innocent is important! It is a matter of being human and sincere. Mirjana was wrong to say Serbs obstruct returnees. Roadblocks are created by politicians.'

Zoran always had to speak his mind immediately. Whenever he did this our immediate fear was that he wanted to leave the project, but once he had expressed his anger he smiled, hugged us and felt even more inspired to continue.

Azra Pasalic gave us the second response. She sat us round the table in her office and offered biscuits, fruit and coffee to lift our spirits.

'Jeff Ford's statement about separating himself from the project did disturb me,' she said. 'We can't count on Serbs now to support us, but good can come out of everything. We need to be fair. Some like Dusan Tubin spoke their stupid views, but the mine management women were on our side. Let's focus on our objective and be tactical in our approach to the mayor. After all, the new mine owners can leave if the situation becomes too dangerous, and lock the doors of the mine again. The mayor would not like that at all!'

The third response came from Graham Day who gave us his assessment of our work at the end of this the second phase of the project, as we sat in the Banja Luka fish restaurant looking sorrowfully into the soup, sick to our stomachs, our appetite gone as we shared our anxiety about Jeff Ford's public withdrawal of support. We feared the group of participants might not be strong enough yet to withstand such a blow. But as Anel already tried to reassure us, this action could be turned to our advantage. The group would survive and persist.

Graham watched us shift bits of fish and vegetable around our plates and became even heartier, his eyes sparkling mischievously but encouragingly above his naval officer's beard. He realized we were at a turning point.

'Don't underestimate what you have done,' he said.

WORKING TOGETHER

RETURN TO OMARSKA

'In three hundred years I shall rise into God's kingdom,' she said.

'You may be able to go before that,' whispered one of the others. 'Invisible we fly through the homes of human beings. They can't see us, so they don't know when we are there. If we find a good person who makes others happy and deserves their love, we smile and God takes a year away from the time of our trial. But if there is evil and meanness in the house we come to, we weep, and for every tear we shed God adds a day to the three hundred years we already must serve.' Conclusion of Hans Christian Andersen's *The Little Mermaid*.

I dreamed vividly before each journey to Bosnia. In this dream I was driving around a city centre, negotiating tricky traffic. I seemed to be carrying my whole home in the back of the car. I spoke with two friendly women, one from Odense in Denmark, and gave them my only address card. The journey became ever more difficult as I tried to reach a place that seemed to be Versailles, the Sun King's palace, with no idea why I had to go there. Trying to avoid the traffic I tangled with one-way systems and found myself going down a narrow street in the wrong direction.

Waking up I realized immediately that Hans Christian Andersen was born in Odense and thought of the last lines of his fairytale, *The Little Mermaid*: the tears for humanity prolonging our time in Purgatory, and these then reminded me of Frederick Hosmer's hymn about the kingdom of God:

Thy kingdom come! On bended knee
The passing ages pray;
And faithful souls have yearned to see
On earth that kingdom's day.

But the slow watches of the night
Not less to God belong;

And for the everlasting right
The silent stars are strong.

And lo, already on the hills
The flags of dawn appear;
Gird up your loins, ye prophet souls,
Proclaim the day is near:

The day in whose clear-shining light
All wrong shall stand revealed,
When justice shall be throned in might,
And every hurt be healed;

When knowledge, hand in hand with peace,
Shall walk the earth abroad:
The day of perfect righteousness,
The promised day of God

Then I dreamed again of driving along a road in Bosnia where flocks of sheep and herds of cattle kept blocking the road. 'Take care!' came the warning.

We arrived on a chilly October day, dusk falling over the dry cornfields as we crossed the River Sava into Bosnia. The storks had flown, but herons still stood sentinel by streams and birds of prey continued to watch motionlessly from posts in fences along the motorway.

Before the groups began the process of sharing their ideas for the memorial we insisted all the participants visit the mine at Omarska and look at the white house, so they could understand its significance, appearance and where it stood in relation to the mine. This meant that the Serb women from the mine and all the young people from the 'round table' and Info Point would see the white house for the first time.

Under an overcast sky, heavy with grey clouds, Muharem Murselovic stood in front of the white house and told its story of horrors, matter-of-factly as though he had done this all too often, his eyes fixed on the mine buildings ahead of him where groups of miners watched from windows. The women did not know where to look, their eyes full of anguish, occasionally glancing at us as though wishing for us to take them somewhere else far away from what they feared to know, and wanted to forget, the terrible truth about what happened in the midst of their community.

They then gingerly walked with Emsuda Mujagic and Nusreta Sivac around the building and up to the road that marked the boundary on the other side from the mine. Flowers that had been brought on August 6th now dried to straw two months later; plastic wrappings, string and ribbons lay strewn over the ground.

The teenagers from Info Point not knowing how to handle the situation wandered over the field kicking clumps of grass and deliberately turning their backs on the white house, as though it were a place cursed and dangerous.

We kept close company with them, sensitive to their perplexity and mixed feelings. The boys hid their thoughts and emotions. We asked more general questions about their views on the future of their town and they spoke hesitantly about sporting facilities for young people, a roller-skating rink in Prijedor; but this did not mean they were ignoring what they were hearing and seeing at Omarska. From this moment to the end of the conference these youngsters became the most determined, thoughtful and imaginative participants in planning the memorial.

One of them said later: 'If we do not deal with this issue there is no future for Prijedor.'

PLANNING THE MEMORIAL

The group discussions needed a firm framework to focus thoughts and ideas on how the memorial should look. There were three main stipulations, all of them agreed by the participants at the group meetings on our previous visit. Firstly the memorial had to give due honour to those who died. Secondly the memorial should not disturb the working of the mine. Thirdly the memorial needed to be a warning and safeguard that such atrocities never happened again. We added a fourth stipulation, that the memorial should have an international dimension and speak to people all over the world.

The participants should also be aware of two stages to the memorial project: the main event which would take time, perhaps years, and to ensure something would be ready by May the following Spring, so visitors knew a memorial was being planned. A resolution on these two stages could be reached at the conference.

The young people who dominated the first of the three work groups were impatient to start and we provided large sheets of paper, pens for them to sketch their plans. We feared the enormity of the task might inhibit them from having any ideas, but in the event suggestions and considerable detail poured out. It did not matter that the results resembled a suburban cemetery with evergreen trees and statues, cobbled footpaths, plaques on walls and enough material to exhibit inside the white house to fill a museum a hundred times bigger. At least they were working together, listening to each other, arguing and coming to compromises. People would speak then others leaped up and rushed to the sheets of paper pasted to the walls, adding squiggles and words. Only half a year earlier these people had not been meeting or talking to each other. Now they acknowledged the past, the truth revealed and accepted.

Issues emerged quickly, common to all the work groups, centring on attitudes to fear and hatred. Would the memorial be inflammatory, inciting violence? Was the white house a museum or a memorial? How could names be recorded? Who would take care of the memorial and decide what went on inside the white house?

The second workshop meeting pitted Emsuda Mujagic against Rezak Hukanovic in the company of a bemused group of young Serbs from Info Point. Emsuda had already decided on several memorial statues including a gigantic weeping bird in a several metre high cage to be sited outside the white house. A sculptor from Bihac had prepared some designs. Rezak shook his head in dismay. These two survivors differed in many ways though sharing a steely resolve, fearless in confronting their persecutors, demanding justice and rights and displaying remarkable courage just by returning to live in their former homes. Rezak doubted that Emsuda could have any useful ideas to contribute. However, when the project almost collapsed shortly before the conference, it was Emsuda's strength of will and far-sightedness that saved the day. Perhaps their similarity of character irked Rezak. He considered Emsuda's proposal to be grotesquely sentimental and inappropriate, confirming his opinion that she could not be taken seriously. To be fair to the sculptor, he had not been to Omarska. Had he seen the white house he would immediately have realized these sculptures would not fit there. Niki paced around the room burdened by the family guilt concerning his brother-in-law's part in the Mount Vlasic massacre. A youth leader of Info Point made a drawing of the memorial site including all Emsuda Mujagic's proposals, helped by one of the teenagers who had performed a popular comic turn in the satirical Wolf and Water theatre piece. The young actor took an intense interest in the project, his face that had made audiences laugh now expressive of serious purpose. Both the actor and the youth leader would eventually make a video of the presentation of the memorial project. They intially feared even looking at let alone entering the white house, but soon they would explore every corner, pointing cameras in all directions, intending to make a historical record for the future.

The third workshop included the women from the mine management, more young people from Info Point, Zoran Ergerac from the Round Table, Boris Danovic, and the only Croat participant Mirjana Verhabovic. Azra Pasalic and Mirsad Duratovic, a survivor from the white house, were the only Bosniaks present. The women from the mine management presented their proposal for a memorial: a path leading from the public road to the white house, closing the place off from the mine, and putting a small plaque by the door. The perfunctory nature of this proposal, delivered in a peremptory manner, inhibited discourse between both sides.

This meeting raised doubts about the possibility of achieving consensus. Zoran Ergerac who normally spoke freely at 'round table' meetings felt intimidated by the presence of so many from the mine management. Also Boris Danovic seemed more reserved, saying: 'We must not have any more trips around the mine. I need to avoid being seen by the workers who complained about the last visit.' He reported that Mayor Marko Pavic had told him he would obstruct the project. It surprised us to discover that Boris Danovic and the mayor were close friends. Boris promised to arrange a private meal where we could talk with the mayor informally. Whenever we bumped into the mayor outside his office he always smiled politely, seeming genuinely pleased to see us, so we reckoned that in a more relaxed environment we might persuade him to accept the project. The mayor eventually agreed to our invitation, and arranged a special lunch for us on Mount Kozara, shortly before the conference.

At the workshop Mirsad Duratovic did not allow the women's modest proposal to upset him and he spoke freely, talking about his experiences and present problems. He even agreed with the women that the memorial should be minimal and without clutter. However he pointed out that the place needed to express the horror of what happened, proposing the presence of one of the trucks that took away the bodies. We were brainstorming, so all these ideas, however flawed or inappropriate could be aired.

Mirjana Verhabovic wanted to turn the white house into a museum, but like Emsuda Mujagic's sculptor, she had not visited the place yet, so did not realize the lack of space for artefacts. She suggested a video installation showing films. 'We cannot have computers in the white house,' was Mirsad Duratovic's shocked response.

Despite the variety of attitudes to the memorial at all three workshops, several basic features were agreed: that the place should be fenced off, a path laid to approach the white house from the road and the white house turned into the memorial. They had different ideas about sculptures, trees and landscape features, fountains and benches. One proposed an eternal flame, keeping the memorial lit at night, another wanted to mark names and numbers of the dead, using the four elements, and keeping the place silent out of respect for those who were killed there. They agreed to call on professional help, hopefully paid for by the mine. We suggested that the path be a labyrinth, addressing the problem how one approaches a place like the white house, not directly, but with due respect. As we kept reminding them, ground on which innocent blood has been spilled is sacred ground. Given the quantity and variety of sculptures and the nature of the land, flat with views of the mine on one side and Mount Kozara on the other they called for a landscape specialist to advise on layout and how best to use the space. The boundary would become a major feature of the memorial, not just a fence or barrier. It needed to be carefully designed and constructed so visitors could see through to the mine and those other buildings where people had suffered. The white house presented the biggest problem. How could an undistinguished building with such a terrible history be made into a memorial? Everyone agreed, however, that its mediocrity was an essential feature and we needed to find an artist able to express the white house's significance, working closely with those who survived the atrocities committed there.

Their imagination fired, the workshops formed groups to discuss each feature of the memorial, its appearance with path and boundary, deciding on statues and landscaping. All agreed that only survivors should decide on the interior of the white house, and the mine management would deal with issues of security and access.

THE PEOPLE OF OMARSKA AND THE MINE
The mediation process had to take into account all people in the area, including the community of the village of Omarska, a mix of poor people whom time seemed to have forgotten and a few rich influential business men and politicians who controlled the municipality of Prijdor. Omarska represented Mayor Marko Pavic's power base, yet the poorer people were neglected by the municipality and complained at being ignored by the mine. To ensure the security of the memorial we needed Omarska to be part of the

project, and after thorough research, Anel and Zoran found Mr Delic, a local businessman, who was prepared to meet us. He owned the Europa Restaurant at Zeljograd at the turning to Omarska.

'Three hundred and fifty Serbs were killed in the Second World War at Kozarac,' Mr Delic told us over coffee at his smart restaurant, just one of several businesses he owned. 'They were buried in an unmarked grave.' He did not explain they were partisan victims of Germans and the Croat Fascist Ustashi, not of the Bosniaks who lived there. This fudging of history continued to stoke resentments and inter-ethnic hatreds. 'I begged my friends not to start a war, but they said the war could not be stopped. It is counter-productive to have memorials anywhere in this region. To prevent unnecessary animosity, no business company should be involved. People here are reserved and docile. What happened, happened. The poorest now suffer most. It is a shame that the diaspora Bosniaks returning on August 6th came into conflict with the Serb wedding party. I had no idea about your work. The Serbs here feel neglected by the international community. Bosniaks are more demanding, stronger and pushier. It bothers me this constant campaign against Serbs. It is inflammatory on both sides. Take the case of Sarajevo, the concentration camp there. It will diffuse the situation if there are as few memorials as possible. At Jasenovac they built a memorial, but the world paid no attention, and it did not stop the last war. The mine should employ more local people. The fact that people think Omarska was a concentration camp in the war does not help the situation. But the people here were not responsible for the camp.' He avoided telling us that people from Omarska worked as guards while the mine operated as a killing camp.

Employment mattered more than memorials to these people. Helping them to deal with this issue might improve the atmosphere and persuade the Serbs there to at least tolerate if not actually support a memorial to Bosniaks. The mine needed to relate to the people, and we offered to set up meetings with the mine management, to begin discussions on how each could help the other.

Mr Delic looked mollified, touched at our patience and sincerity, not yet understanding that there can be no progress in peace mediation if all sides are not being brought along at the same time. He agreed to set up another meeting with more business people from Omarska. As a successful businessman he approved of stability in the region, and for that reason had only contempt for politicians. He proposed a meeting between the communities of Omarska and Kozarac, a significant event if we managed to arrange it, considering recent history.

DECIDING TOGETHER

TEARS AND FIGHTS

Our visit to Bosnia in November coincided with riots erupting in France, disaffected Muslim youths setting Paris on fire. Just before we left on our July visit, three Muslim suicide bombers had killed fifty two people in London.

This stage of the project turned out to be the hardest. We had several arguments with our management team, the two people we most relied on to make it work. The 'round table' fractured, former friends and allies, like Kemal Pervanic, became our adversaries, and Mayor Marko Pavic persistently blocked us. Mediation process expects these problems. The participants themselves rescued the project by focusing on deciding and agreeing the memorial.

The presence of a film team, In Focus Productions, chronicling our progress also disturbed the process, though in the end the director Alison Rooper's dogged persistence and sympathy for the project helped give confidence to the participants, as we had hoped. But Anel and Zoran resented her presence. 'She is only doing this for herself,' they said, 'and getting in the way of the project. This is difficult and dangerous work, and she could ruin our efforts.' Their opinion mattered to us, constantly aware of the perils of this project, especially to both of them. The reputation of the media in Bosnia is summed up in the film *No Mans Land*. Everyone suspected foreign media of profiting from other people's suffering.

The mine manager told us: 'The majority of the people here are against the white house being a memorial. The mayor will destroy it!' He insisted we needed more time. The mine women too warned us that we had to get the mayor on our side. 'We do have difficulties,' one of them said, understating the case. 'But from the beginning I made up my mind and am consistent.'

The groups divided as expected: the mine management having given their opinions about the memorial restricted their attention to matters of security and access. Boris Danovic continued to cooperate on all matters concerning the site of the memorial, but he failed to attend a number of meetings, being called away on business in Germany. The young people of Info Point and the 'round table' worked with survivors on how the memorial should look, while the survivors of Omarska discussed what should happen in the white house itself. All agreed that whatever design came out of the discussions would be no more than a proposal. They acknowledged that after the conference they needed to call on professional help and involve more people in the project.

Edin Ramulic had been whipping up hostility to us on the internet from the diaspora and we began to receive angry phone calls from Kemal Pervanic. Emsuda Mujagic's son, Sadko, another Omarska survivor, who now lived in Rotterdam, demanded to know the names of all participants in the project. Though we kept inviting Kemal and Sadko to come and take part, they objected to Serb involvement. Edin Ramulic told them about us meeting regularly with the mayor. They did not understand that we were trying to ensure the security of the memorial. We always knew the diaspora to be an important element in the project, and planned to engage their cooperation once the mediation process had achieved a secure foothold, after the presentation.

The survivors of the white house, Rezak Hukanovic and Mirsad Duratevic, met with the two survivors of Omarska, Nusreta Sivac and Muharem Murselovic, in Muharem Murselovic's office. All looked tired and in need of encouragement.

Muharem Murselovic yawned and launched into a speech: 'We need to tear down barriers and walls and find a balance. There are extreme radical views on all sides. Some people say nothing happened, others that the whole mine be turned into a memorial. We have to find a sensible balance. And it shouldn't be minimal. The white house was only part of the concentration camp, but it represents everything that happened. How do we achieve what we intend in such a banal building? The space can be purposefully used, with pictorial displays in all four rooms, models, miniatures, photos from the exhumation, lists of people who were killed, bits and pieces of clothes, pictures of the murderers. Horror is important. Visitors have to go out with a feeling of what happened there. But there might be other solutions. The Berlin Reichstag Memorial manages to reflect on German history, its leaders and wars. The enclosed space has music. People can enter the picture. It is authentic and theatrical with powerful plastic and visual qualities.'

We asked whether they thought the white house could carry all that; was it big enough to be a museum?

'Everything has to be for the survivors,' said Nusreta Sivac. 'What happened has to be depicted authentically, in all the rooms, including those in other buildings. There should be no fence or barrier between the white house and other parts of the mine where women were held. The view must not be blocked. This means a lot to the women who suffered there. There should be testimonies in the white house, personal effects, belongings, photos of mass graves, bit and pieces of survivors. Among the remains at the first exhumation they found a letter from a murdered victim to his Serb wife. The letter is well preserved, despite being buried for years with the body. These details are important so visitors can experience more closely what happened.'

The major issue of the memorial's appearance focused on how to express so much in such a small space. 'It is a question of size and being able to say everything inside,' mused Mirsad Duratovic. 'Personally I am against audio visual devices. What will stop a person in his tracks? Maybe it is a shirt or a piece of clothing. Is the white house the right place for this? So many bits and pieces, all important, need to be placed inside in some form, implements of torture, cables, weapons, pictures of criminals, models of the entire camp, the bucket used for washing hands after killing.'

'I am a journalist and deal with facts,' said Rezak Hukanovic.'I am also a writer and artist. We need to find a synthesis of these solutions. We share the same views and I am thinking of how to arrange the tiny space with miniature models of the mine, photos of criminals on the walls, displaying belongings. These must include the chess board and decks of cards made from scraps of paper, the purpose being to play and blot out reality, the screams, the shouting and beatings. Visitors have to experience the horror when they enter. We could have speakers inside the white house playing the names of the victims in a perpetual loop, mixed with shouts and music. Maybe all this needs to be in a separate building with videos and other material. The place has to be silent. People who enter need to show respect. All comments must be made after leaving the white house.'

Mirsad Duratovic considered the audio installation to be distracting, then made an important observation which changed the way everyone had so far been thinking about turning the white house into a memorial: not only did it have insufficient space to contain all the material, it was also too small for visitors. Artefacts and material would constrict the space further. Access needed to be restricted, only a few people going inside at a time.

We pointed out that specialists in installations could be called in to design the interior, minimal in appearance yet containing all the material. If done with imagination and skill, the white house could become a profoundly moving memorial.

Discussing the security and access to the memorial with the women from the mine management at the mine headquarters, Boris Danovic felt that walking to the white house should in itself be a mark of respect: 'The way you go around it must be subtle and delicate. There has to be a marking, step by step. I will guarantee a method of doing this that will persuade the doubters. The white house has to be physically separate from the rest of the mine, and I can help with that too. I am also ready to present my part of the project at the conference, but do not want to be interviewed or filmed. This is not because I am afraid, but because people know who I am and that could distract attention from the project. It is imperative that we build up Serb support from Omarska.'

'Thirty six women were raped and tortured in Omarska,' Emsuda Mujagic told us at the workshop where the exterior appearance of the memorial was being considered. 'We must take into account other buildings where people suffered apart from the white house. In the fullness of time all the buildings will be part of the memorial. We need to give the mine owners leeway and time to relocate their administration at the mine.'

Mayor Marko Pavic had insisted on our first meeting in May that there should be no more memorials built in Bosnia. We knew he meant a ban on memorials to Bosniaks, not to Serbs. So we were not surprised to discover that a week before we arrived back at Prijedor he had attended the opening of another memorial to Serb war dead in Omarska, a different one to that already standing next to the Trnopolje concentration camp. At the ceremony, given prominence in the Republika Srpska media, he gave a speech denouncing all attempts at reconciliation. 'These people died for the Republika Srpska!' he declared.

Telling us about the ceremony at Omarska, Azra Pasalic's eyes filled with tears and anger when we met next in her office. 'My father was in Omarska. My son wanted to see where he had been held. He did not die there but was killed afterwards. We need to preserve the place in such a way that it speaks a message for the future. We need to record the words and testimonies of all survivors so that it never happens again in the future.'

'The mayor has become more extreme,' Muharem Murselovic told us when we met him in Banja Luka at the National Assembly. 'He is seen as being the defender of Serb interests, a guardian of the Republika Srpska. Now his party is more extreme than the SDS, who as you know are extreme enough already.' The SDS, (Srpska Demokratska Stranka, Srpska Democratic Party) established by Radovan Karadjic, was in power. Murselovic continued: 'my party has actually more members in the Assembly than the mayor's, but only he is invited to top level consultations with the international community.'

Despite the hardening of attitudes by the top nationalist politicians in Bosnia, and the constant support given them by the international community, people were now voicing less extreme attitudes, even in Omarska which had provided most of the guards at the killing camp. Women on the Omarska Council addressed the Prijedor Assembly, expressing dismay at the negative image of their community because of the killing camp. 'We are not responsible for what happened, but the criminals should be punished and we be allowed to get on with our future,' they said.

Muharem Murselovic considered politicians crucial in initiating this change of heart, perhaps being one himself. 'Watch out for a trap,' he warned about Mr Delic's proposed meeting between the communities of Serb Omarska and Bosniak Kozarac. 'We can't easily reconcile. First we need justice and the punishment of the guilty. I know Bosniaks who socialise with Serbs and say they are nice people. What do they actually talk about? The weather? Certainly they don't talk about the bad things that happened. I am always unpopular for raising issues of the past. We have to cleanse the past in order to move into the future. The failure of Communism taught me that lesson: not to sweep issues under the carpet. When the system collapsed, ghouls and monsters emerged. Serbs can only come on board if they start to speak candidly. The Serbs were police officers, soldiers, miners and guards, always part of the system; that's their mindset. They feel the need to conform to the system, and few will oppose their political leaders. So now we need our top politicians to take the lead and say: we have to support the vulnerable people. Mayor Pavic won't do it. Maybe Republika Srpska President Cavic can be persuaded.'

Having spoken so negatively about Mayor Marko Pavic it came as a surprise to us that Muharem Murselovic had invited the mayor to a Bajram celebration at Cordas, and even more of a surprise that the mayor turned up.

Alison Rooper of In Focus Productions filmed the event, being present there by chance. This film and a mass of photographs showed the two men sitting side by side, both politicians, former school friends whose lives had taken different paths. The mayor smiles confident in his power; Muharem Murselovic beams with pride, raising glasses and leading the group in raucous singsongs. On the one hand the film depicts a united community, sharing a meal, carousing together, on the other it is a chilling reminder of home videos made before the Bosnia War, also showing Serbs and Bosniak neighbours celebrating together. The Serbs talk openly to camera of the inevitability of ethnic cleansing. Then the massacres began.

Meanwhile the young Serbs from Info Point and the Bosniak survivors continued to work on the concept of the memorial.

'We are dancing a ballet on ice,' commented the mine director when we met to update on the project's progress. 'It is impossible not to fall over! The mayor and municipality have to agree to the project. My objective is to create a positive ambient atmosphere.'

He felt the time had come to involve those who had initiated the mediation process, his bosses in Holland and London. They responded by agreeing to send representatives to the conference that we had now booked for December.

More significantly the mine director and the three women from the mine management promised to support the memorial to its completion.

'We are aboard with the project, and are not afraid,' one of them reassured us. 'The municipality and the public may say the mine is doing all this, but they misunderstand. We need to bring more people on line. The white house should stay intact and made into the memorial and our task is to provide access and security.'

'I was suspicious of the project at first,' said another. 'I knew it would be difficult. To a certain extent I am happy with the working groups, and have no difficulty talking to different people and hearing other opinions. I come aboard as an individual, not as a representative of the mine. I represent my own feelings and not those of other workers here. Looking back over the last few months you made big progress. However you need more people to accept the project, the municipality and all communities'

'If we run into roadblocks we must tell people that we are making a new beginning,' said the first mine woman. 'If people say it's not happening elsewhere, we have to tell them we are starting here first. Maybe we moved too fast too far, being such a sensitive issue. More time needs to be given.'

'People should be grateful for this memorial, whatever it is,' commented Mirjana Verhabovic, the only Croat participant of the memorial project. 'Everyone will have their own memories.'

She attended Bajram with Muharem Murselovic and Mayor

Marko Pavic, and can be seen on the film lustily joining in the singing.

She liked the idea of a labyrinth, with its sacred connotations that transcended religious differences, and reminded us that for decades of communism in the former Yugoslavia, people, especially the Bosniaks, paid little attention to religious matters.

'It is ludicrous to have a memorial for just one religious group,' she said. 'After the Second World War, Bosniaks did not visit cemeteries. Their religion says: bury and leave, which gave rise to the traditional saying here in Bosnia: Turks run away from graveyards! Only after the recent war did Bosniaks start to visit cemeteries. They were never as pious as the Catholics. The labyrinth is a good idea.' Then she added with a mischievous smile and wink: 'Teach these Bosniaks how to respect the dead! My husband was a Muslim, but not practising. I kept his gravestone in the garage but people thought the Serbs had destroyed it. As to the lack of interest in Croatia for victims of Omarska, considering the great number of victims, I blame Bishop Komarica. He should have returned the people to Prijedor. And he was nominated for the Nobel Peace Prize! People did not leave Prijedor by choice, they were killed or they fled. After what Tudjman did, the Croats want to forget about the war. They also carried out ethnic cleansing, of Serbs and Bosniaks. They don't want to remember crimes against themselves because they don't want to be reminded of their crimes against others. Now we live in a time when people excuse their crimes by blaming them on tensions. Communists are still in power, dressed up as the new nationalists. No one abides by the laws. This leads to apathy and envy of those who get rich by crime. There is no Tito to put these criminals in their place, no belief in God, and democracy is in its infancy here. Only the other day I went for a pizza at a place owned by friends from the old days; they were Serbs but did not take part in the war and remained sane. A customer saw me and stood up, half drunk, shouting at them: 'How dare you serve a returnee!' He had taken part in the killing, and anyone serving Catholics or Bosniaks is considered a bad Serb. I turned to the owners and asked: Am I welcome? Am I safe? If not, you should put on your door: No Croats, No Dogs! After that I had no more trouble. Every returnee has to defend himself, and remain.'

She concluded by observing that the memorial should not whip up ghosts from the past, and added with a laugh: 'I am in favour of a labyrinth; educate these peasants and savages!'

The mayor and the municipality were making their opposition to the memorial publicly known. The mine director's wife advised us to form a sub-committee, including herself, which could help steer the memorial plans through the town council where those hostile to the project would place obstacles in its path. All the participants acknowledged the formidable difficulties we faced, but seemed determined to continue, fearless and steadfast.

The young people wanted to meet more frequently, even without our presence. 'We are wasting time in useless discussions; as a group we have to work more,' said one of the young people, a feisty Serb girl from Prijedor. 'We produced four drawings at our last meetings, but none of them were there to look at, the workshop went down the plughole.' This had not been an oversight on our part but an attempt to take the ideas forward, concentrating on what had been basically agreed rather than on details, on the space around the white house, within it and the boundary rather than continuing disagreements about sculptures. The feisty girl said: 'Many people have ludicrous ideas. You can't relocate administration buildings; the new mine owners didn't have anything to do with what happened. It is absurd to disrupt the mine work for small visits. And I disagree with inflammatory symbols. Old people can hold on to these feelings, but the young must not perpetuate them.'

'We need to raise awareness in people,' said a young man, a sporty youth leader, 'point out the sufferings of people so it never happens again, and help people understand and open their eyes. The memorial should speak for itself when people visit. No weapons, no instruments of torture, nothing explicit.'

At this point the project ran into more problems.

First Anel and Zoran complained about Alison Rooper and the

filming, which began to interfere with their arrangements. Bosnians are notoriously difficult to pin down, and any success at getting people to attend meetings was entirely due to Anel's persistence on the phone, calling on the hour, cajoling, reminding and reminding again. The presence of cameras and new faces to deal with made people nervous. War carried on in Bosnia, not overtly, but quietly and destructive of personal lives, so mediation became a delicate balancing act, hoping not to inflame a situation, building trust on both sides. The film threatened to expose people. People went along with Alison Rooper's demands, which meant hours repeating their speeches, time that played havoc with our management team's schedule. She managed to charm most participants. Mayor Marko Pavic even lent her his official car and driver to the airport when she left. But Anel and Zoran did not trust her motives and disliked being kept waiting. Even Misha, our affable Serb driver who never had a bad word to say about anyone, lost his temper with her. She tried to get him to drive her to distant villages and in the end he put his foot down: 'Please lady! I work for the project! I have no time for this!'

Anel and Zoran's stress also stemmed from complicated decisions and plans concerning the presentation. We changed our mind several times about the venue. First we had hoped to bring everyone to England, out of Bosnia. We were not sure however if the mayor would have been granted a visa, because of questions about his past. A crucial element in the project, we needed him to support the memorial. We then considered using a hotel on Mount Vlasic, ideal for high-level consultations because of its isolation, so remote and inaccessible that participants could not leave or come and go as they pleased. But would they turn up at all? We drove to the hotel, passing the rock where Niki's brother in law had taken part in the massacre of dozens of Bosniak men and boys during the war. Situated in the Federation and not in the Republika Srpska where Serbs felt more secure, the mine management and the mayor were unlikely to come there.

On the drive back we stopped to drink coffee at an isolated guest house by the River Ugar, half way through the Vlasic wilderness, forest covered mountains rearing up on all sides, the nearest habitation many miles away. A bear caught locally slumbered in a cage; a wolf in another cage further down the valley. The guest house owner, a Bosniak refugee in Germany who had returned home with his son, winked in a friendly manner when we asked to see the bear, took beer from the fridge, led us to the cage and rattled the wire mesh with the bottle. The massive bear rose from his stupor and loped towards the desired refreshment, sitting on his hind haunches, seizing the beer with both paws, head back and emptied the bottle at a single draft. The bear of Vlasic reminded us of the mayor and we proceded on our journey, deciding to have the presentation at the Atina Hotel in Banja Luka.

'You have to know, I love details,' said Zoran, emphasising the last three words, and set about organizing a conference that went like clockwork. He drew up lists, employed four assistants to help in the office, and turned into a martinet, focusing on the smallest detail, whether it be pens and stationary, folders, times of meals, lay out of the room, order of events, the needs of each participant, and attending keenly to every likely problem that could arise: disruption from dissenters, varied transport for different people, security at the hotel, interpreters, police guards, etc. Zoran turned out to be adept at striking bargains and getting what he wanted. At last we met the owner of the Atina Hotel, rotund and beaming in baggy trousers and sweat shirt like a garage mechanic, only too eager to cooperate and host this conference of Serbs and Bosniaks, not at all the cool intimidating tough guy in Rayburns we were expecting, allegedly one of the leading gangsters in Banja Luka.

Meanwhile at the workshops some participants became restless.

Zoran Ergarac, a lecturer in economics at a business institute run by a wealthy entrepreneur in Prijedor, and part-time inter-preter at the mine headquarters, took us aside to warn us about the mine management being the chief opposition to the project. 'Your memorial is way over the horizon!' he told us.

We had initially felt ill at ease in the mine headquarters, but gained the trust of key people there: the women from the mine management, engineers and many workers at Omarska. For this reason we poured all energies into strengthening their commitment, and above all encouraging their awareness that the future of the mine and the whole region depended on them participating in the presentation at the conference.

Anger, fear and impatience erupted at the next workshop meeting. Rezak Hukanovic launched an attack on us, implying that he had no more interest in the project and that there would be no presentation because the memorial was being used for propaganda purposes, and he wanted no part in that game. Rather than enter a futile argument, sensing that only the participants, especially the survivors, had a right to speak, we left the room. Emir our interpreter followed us and in his usual perspicacious way calmed us down explaining with a smile: 'This is typical Bosnian behaviour and everything will be fine, you'll see. People need to express their feelings, they shout and hit out all over the place, but then come to their senses.' We listened to the table inside the room being thumped, more shouts, then suddenly Emsuda Mujagic's voice being raised in a headmistressy way followed by what seemed like silence. This persisted for half an hour. They were quietly discussing how to take the project forward. The door opened and the sheepishly smiling sporty youth leader from Info Point beckoned us inside. The atmosphere had changed completely. Tensions and stress transformed into calm reasonable conversation. Emsuda Mujagic had read them the riot act, pointing out that they could not squander this unique opportunity of creating a memorial at Omarska.

The issue now became clear: without a presentation at the conference the Soul of Europe's work ended; there would be no memorial and prospects of future trouble and disruptions. However, with a presentation the Soul of Europe might be permitted to stay on, help create the memorial, and develop further mediation between the people, the mine and the different communities. So the participants agreed to prepare a presentation. They would do this on their own without our presence.

'These groups have no real authority,' explained Rezak Hukanovic later. 'We are not entitled to speak for everyone, there are too few of us. There will be many questions at the presentation. The issue is that the momentum for the project slumped, not because of us or you, but because of politics. Everyone noticed something important was happening. The mayor came out publicly against the project. We have to find a solution so even though there are many differences of opinions and ideas, Emsuda and I will never agree for instance, we have to make a presentation to the mine and to the mine owners.'

The meeting ended peacefully and in good spirits.

Though Emsuda Mujagic single-handedly held the project together just as it seemed to fracture, the men did not acknowledge her skills.

'There is animosity between Emsuda and Rezak,' said Muharem Murselovic afterwards. 'But Rezak is more qualified to speak, being directly involved. Emsuda is a woman who does not understand things. But I respect her need to take part and express her views, which are a bit mysterious to me. The mayor however is a bigger concern because everything depends upon him. He is devious and demoniacal. If only someone could relieve him of his duties, sack him! He will subvert the project. Recently the mayors of Travnik and Skender Vakuf met to discuss a memorial where on August 1992 two hundred and fifty young men were murdered.' These towns were in the Federation, Skender Vakuf close to Mount Vlasic. Murselovic continued: 'Some of the killers came from Prijedor.' He was referring to the massacre in which Niki's brother-in-law had taken part. 'One of them, Darko Mrjen, led the squad that did the murders and confessed to the crimes at the Hague Tribunal. He gave the names of others involved. He now has a seventeen year sentence. The mayors met and agreed on a memorial. I told Mayor Pavic about it and asked why he hadn't attended the meeting. "I will pay for the memorial," he said, "the only important thing is that it mustn't be in Prijedor", this despite so many killers coming from there. "All that matters is that it isn't here!" he told me. "Get buses to take people to Manjaca or wherever the memorial is."'

Suddenly overwhelmed by emotion Muharem Murselovic let out all his frustration and despair concerning the mayor: 'He is a dangerous man, he cuts support for the returnee process, lies about the status of refugees and persistently works to conceal crimes he was actively engaged in. He hid behind the protection of a security agency. He did visit Omarska while it was a concentration camp but wants to hush this up. He still works for the same Serbia Montenegrin security agency. He keeps a tight grip around Prijedor. He is able to reign in all parties. All are under his control!'

Muharem Murselovic climaxed his attack on the mayor by screaming in despair: 'You ask me: what is the main problem in Prijedor? He the mayor is the main problem!'

'Don't count on the diaspora,' he told us, on hearing of our problems with stressful phonecalls from abroad. 'They are far away and don't understand the situation. They use the Prijedor situation to their own ends. They want this to be a region without hope. The diaspora keep telling me that we must support the Bosniak army. They come to see the site of the battle of Sanski Most, then go home again and find reasons never to return. If they want a memorial they must come back and work with us.'

'As for the former mine manager who is now helping this project, I have to tell you that in 1992 he gave the seam over to the authorities and permitted the use of buildings for interrogation, torture and killing, also transport of bodies to places like Jacarina Koza where three hundred and seventy four people were buried in a mass grave. They were buried with skill so a team of experts from the mine must have been in charge. In the war people just jumped on the bandwagon.'

'If I shared Rezak's views I would probably have left the project long ago and done something else,' one of the young leaders from Info Point told us. 'This is the way people behave here, but I think you deserved more respect. I will give as much time as necessary to the project. Political games must not enter. As a young man who has to live here I will contribute as much as possible to get it right. We are not a political party. As I told you from the beginning, the most important thing is the truth. The European Union ambassador came to Info Point a few weeks ago saying: the future belongs to you, the youth. I contradicted him and told him: No, you are wrong, it is the present that should belong to us.'

The European Union ambassador took an interest in Info Point for being a coalition of youth non-governmental organizations, all chipping in with funds raised by one of the few international non-governmental organizations still running in Prijedor, the Local Democracy Agency. Info Point acted as a resource centre for the whole region, supplying information and helping young people in the countryside as well as the town. They constantly tried and failed to raise funds from the municipality. Funds were pledged but the mayor blocked them, now that he had found out they were involved in the memorial project.

Like the Serbs from the 'round table', these brave young people had made themselves vulnerable to attack by involving themselves in the project. They had not come on board for reward. The future of their home town mattered more.

Zeljko Kantar, another brave Serb, a social worker in his late thirties, had been attacked for being a traitor. When Anel returned from America, Zeljko had gone out of his way to look after him, taking him to cafes – and brothels even, though we hesitated to ask about those. Anel called him 'Anzeljko' ('angelic') for being so supportive. 'He had no friends,' Zeljko Kantar told us at the Restaurant Le Pont. 'One day we visited Omarska. Former guards recognized me and came round to my workplace asking what I was doing there. They are still ignorant about the new owners wanting to clear the name of the mine. Both sides need to be concerned. My opinion is that we must wrap up what happened in the past and head for Europe. We have to deal with the killing camps and look to the future. I can liaise between you and the people in Omarska. You need to meet more Christians here. As Anglicans you can be a stepping stone to the Orthodox.'

Our Anglicanism had helped on our first project in Bosnia, getting the Orthodox and Catholic bishops to meet with Bosniaks in Coventry in 2001.

'Anglicans are respected by both sides,' Zeljko continued. 'The mayor refuses to countenance a Bosniak memorial at Omarska. He was born there. His people are there.' Then looking at the waiters hovering around our table he added: 'The waiters here will report me to the mayor. Don't worry. I will tell them you are giving me a million euros. They will be speechless. Life has improved in Prijedor but on days of high risk, football matches for instance, people waver and follow the mob blindly, not caring about breaking the law. I spend all my time with the poor and the lowest classes. You need to understand the souls of the people. Visitors and politicians don't. So the poor get used to just being objects of pity.'

Nusreta Sivac remained optimistic throughout this, the stormiest passage of the project, telling us: 'I am happy because the project is going in a positive direction. We have to wrap it up in a positive way. Future visits to the mine will have a different meaning, once the place is marked. I am particularly pleased that something will have been done for those who died, also the survivors. Those who died have not been forgotten. I bear a heavy moral burden because I survived only by chance. I could have been in one of those mass graves. The memorial will be a civilized gesture of enormous significance. Survivors are aware of it being sited in an ethnically cleansed environment.'

She went on: 'People need to acknowledge what happened so the memorial can have a broader significance, not just for those who died. People in other parts of Bosnia where horrors happened can do what we are doing. I am happy to hear that the mayor of Travnik is allowed to raise a memorial on another mass grave. He has President Tihic's support from the Federation, and also from mayors in the Republika Srpska. What we are doing will change the thinking and attitudes of all people. We are approaching Europe and need to meet civilized standards. Not only did people suffer and die, but a system of values collapsed. Everyone thought each was right. We have to carry out a revision of ourselves. To be honest I didn't think this project would become so important. Owing to you it did. Had we tried to do it locally it would have ended in arguments and vicious circles. Lack of understanding would have deepened. Survivors agree this is a big event, especially those who haven't been here since 1992.'

Her comment on civilized values reminded us that these had broken down across the world, not just in Bosnia. Nusreta Sivac's observation that each side believed in its rightness, even claiming God's support, could be seen all the way from the West to East. This kind of mediation, on the ground, bringing all sides together, making them talk, persisting, never giving up, seemed to her and us the only alternative for the future.

'Talking with the women from the mine,' Nusreta Sivac went on thoughtfully, answering our request that she and Emsuda Mujagic make more efforts to meet and socialize with them, 'maybe they think it is premature. It is difficult to accept the truth of what happened and therefore they fear a backlash from their constituency. I listen to many Serbs who despite the dangers nevertheless approached and helped Bosniaks, and now pride themselves on their courage. We can be supportive and we should help other ethnic groups' projects. We must not fear being condemned by those who can't bring themselves to acknowledge what happened.'

THE MAYOR OF PRIJEDOR ON MOUNT KOZARA

The mayor invited us for lunch with Graham Day. He had reserved a table at the restaurant Bijelo Voda, one of Tito's many residences in the former Yugoslavia. It was situated on Mount Kozara, next to the memorial to partisans killed in the Second World War.

We guessed the significance of this choice of venue. The mayor wanted us to understand the exceptionally bloody history of this region of Europe from his Serb nationalist perspective.

We were genuine in our thanks for this invitation. It gave us a unique opportunity to hear his defence of ethnic cleansing and continuation of the cycle of violence endemic in Bosnia. The gloom and dankness of the pine forests in late autumn recalled images of Hitler and Third Reich war leaders meeting in a similarly dark and remote part of a Prussian forest, the Wolf's Lair, to plan the invasion of Russia, a war on all fronts in Europe and the destruction of the Jewish race.

The mayor arrived in a black Mercedes with two intimidating colleagues who remained silent throughout the lunch, one of them Dusan Tubin, chairman of the mayor's cabinet.

Graham Day immediately landed a couple of punches before the lunch started, in order to pre-empt any hostilities from the mayor. 'The mine owners might chose another iron-ore mine in Romania to feed Zenica if this mediation process is not supported,' he began. 'Then the region will ignite like a powder keg.' We added that there were already dangers and threats from the diaspora. The mayor, looking momentarily shaken, quibbled feebly about some misreporting about a bomb being thrown through a window of a mosque in Prijedor when in fact it had just been a stone with the word bomb written on it. The bomb went off twenty yards away from the mosque, not actually inside, so he felt the Bosniaks had nothing to complain about. 'Srebrenica already has a memorial,' he went on. 'And now it has all these ethnic tensions. Prijedor has no monument and we have no ethnic tensions. So what's the problem? Why did the mine owners call for this mediation? It isn't necessary. We have excellent relations between all communities.'

Concerning the apparent harmony between the ethnic groups in the region we had long learned not to argue with him. The facts spoke for themselves, but he reckoned by repeating a lie often enough eventually everyone would believe it. However he had to acknowledge to himself, even if not publicly, that Graham Day could be correct about the region being a powder keg. It was just a matter of time, and the memorial project might bring that danger closer. The effect of this conversation had the opposite of what we intended. Far from supporting the project the mayor became more determined than ever to end it as soon as possible: a short-term elimination of a problem to protect his interests.

Graham Day joshed the mayor over the security of his position, warning that if the mayor did not cooperate he would face consequences from the international community. The mayor smiled wanly and said: 'I know you can get rid of me whenever you like.' Though Graham Day smiled back as though implying such a day would never come, the threat remained: a sword of Damocles over Mayor Marko Pavic.

Graham Day then had to leave. We continued in vain to try and improve the attitude of the mayor towards the memorial. Suddenly the mayor looked old and tired. After a generous lunch of chicken soup and steak, washed down with Montenegrin wine and fruit brandy, he lead us up Mount Kozara to show us the memorial, the main purpose of this invitation.

We stood shivering in a light drizzle, mud, murk and the dark forests surrounding the concrete walls inscribed with names of thousands of partisans who died in the battle against fascism. The mayor made no attempt to pick a possibly more suitable spot for his brief speech. We stood and stared at long lists of Bosniak names like Osmanovic and listened to his tragic lie which he still persisted in believing despite the evidence in front of him: 'All these people were Serbs,' he said. 'The message is clear. Now you can tell who our enemies were and who fought on the side of the fascists.'

He then shook our hands, turned away, placed his arms on the shoulder of Dusan Tubin and the other colleague for support and staggered down the hill to his waiting Mercedes.

Our final view of the mayor was of an old man, a once tall powerful frame now bent and fragile, turning his back decisively on us and the project. This spectre from a mythic history that glorified a Greater Serbia and its battle with Islam still held the region in its iron grip.

The two Serb business men we then met in Omarska later that day confirmed the persistence of lie over truth. Mr Delic from the Europa Restaurant at Zeljograd on the way to Omarska had only managed to persuade one other Serb to see us. The other four he had invited were frightened, apparently. 'We need to organize the meeting through the local community,' Mr Delic said, adding: 'To be honest I don't know what to think. I am in two minds and confused.'

The other businessman said no one had been informed about

the meeting. 'Do you really think this memorial will bring reconciliation?' he asked rhetorically. 'I think it is counter-productive.
Most Serbs and Bosniaks are good neighbours and already
building a middle ground to create stability for our children and
grandchildren. This memorial is premature. My house is near the
mine. When the Muslims came to visit in August they ran into a
local wedding procession and assaulted the guests. The police had
to come and protect them.' Already facts were being twisted with
no mention of insults being hurled by the wedding guests telling
the Bosniaks to leave Bosnia or die.

'Omarska was not a concentration camp,' he continued.
'Jasenovac was a concentration camp. Only fifteen or twenty
people died at Omarska. The foreign press were here and know the
facts. Very few were killed there. Most of those who died were
taken away and killed elsewhere. Why should there be a memorial
for only ten or twelve people? The army did it anyway. As a result
Omarska became a symbol of blackness.'

The only way to deal with such rewriting of history, where
even the numbers of the dead were reduced in succeeding
sentences, was to approach the issue from a different angle.

'What can we do for Omarska?' we asked.

He looked surprised and relieved at this sudden change of tack:
'Get public lighting systems from the mine. The mine should
accept its responsibility for the region. The mine should look after
the roads. You have to help improve relations between the mine
and the community. This needs doing before the community can
be expected to cooperate about memorials. The Muslims should
not be inflammatory. Once business runs smoothly then problems
between the communities can ease.'

The discussion took a more positive turn. Concerns about the
condition of Omarska, lack of employment, neglect and poor
relations with the mine mattered more than the memorial.

As the conference date approached, along with the reality of a
presentation about the memorial by Serbs and Bosniaks, some of
the participants became nervous, others more determined. The
older Serbs, like the mine director's wife and Zeljko Skondric, the

one member of the mayor's cabinet who still supported the project though not attending meetings or workshops, kept warning us we would need the mayor's support before work on the memorial could start, and the local council might put obstacles in its way, such as questioning change of use of the land from being an industrial zone to a memorial. But they promised to help steer the project through the council. One of the first tasks after the presentation would be to establish a management committee for the memorial project to deal with these issues.

MIRSAD IN BISCANI

Anel heard that extreme Bosniak nationalists from the SDA party, mostly living in Sanski Most on the Federation side of the region, were angry at not being involved in the project. They could disrupt the presentation. But at a meeting we explained to them the nature of the mediation process, getting people from all sides, especially Serbs, to agree on the basis for a memorial. The conference at which the presentation was the main event gave the project authority and the mine would publicly announce its support for it. After that the diaspora and others who had not yet been involved would be included in the final working out of the memorial. The Bosniak nationalists told their grim stories and seemed relieved to hear they had not been sidelined.

'This is the most do-able among the most difficult projects,' Graham Day told Jeff Ford and Giorgio Blais, a retired Italian general now director of the regional centre of the Organization for Security and Co-operation in Europe (OSCE) Mission to Bosnia in Banja Luka, who had asked to meet us and make peace at the Office of the High Representative's centre in Banja Luka. They had not changed their position but were annoyed by attacks on them in the National Assembly from Muharem Murselovic. Though continuing to be pro-Serb they still wanted the Bosniak community to consider the OSCE neutral. 'Reconciliation starts with civilized dialogue,' Graham continued, as irritated by this meeting as we were, but going through the motions. 'The new mine owners are important to everybody. It is like riding a wobbly bike, no one wants to see you crash. Endeavours like this are not a priority for the OHR on an official basis, so my support is personal. Extremists are growing to a crescendo as the project improves. Now we are starting to hurt. The closer to success we are the worse the acrimony. But opposition can be controlled. There will be a backlash from the diaspora; busloads of traumatized victims came in August. Any rehabilitation of Serbs will cause conflict with these victims and survivors. But any breaking of the law has to be answerable to the police.'

We pointed out that the OSCE's apparent withdrawal of support for the memorial gave heart to the Serbs, took it away from the Bosniaks, encouraged extreme Bosniaks who disapproved of the mediation process and worst of all, put the lives of those Serbs from the mine, the 'round table' and Info Point who were bravely committing themselves publicly to the project at risk. Katerina Panic was now a marked woman and Zeljko Kantar had been told: 'You are a traitor. Watch out!'

'We are in perilous waters,' said Jeff Ford, unimpressed. 'We must not shake the boat.'

'We want reconciliation,' said Giorgio Blais suddenly. He had until then been sitting in a silent stupor.

Graham Day then punched home about Prijedor's grim future, diaspora disrupting the mine next summer, the possibility of the mine owners losing interest in Omarska and preferring to get their iron ore from the Ukraine, Romania, or even China.

After our problems with the OSCE, complaints from the diaspora and warnings about the mine management's opposition to the project, it came as an unexpected relief to meet Mirsad Duratovic in his office at Biscani. Biscani was one of the Bosniak villages, on the way from Prijedor to Sanski Most, destroyed in 1992, the population driven out, many killed.

Mirsad Duratovic along with Rezak Hukanovic had been tortured in the white house and seen his father, brother and uncles killed. Despite these traumas he had a relaxed and friendly manner, often chuckling and always looking for a positive resolution. Every meeting with him was a pleasure.

'Talking to you lightens my spirits,' he told us when we remarked on his surprising good humour, given his past traumas and present difficulties. He explained that he did not like to talk about painful issues at home, his family having suffered so much and wanting to put the past behind them and get on with their lives without being perpetually reminded of horrors. He therefore valued our attention which gave him the opportunity to unburden his soul.

We arrived at Mirsad Duratovic's office in Biscani just as telephone lines were being connected, groups of hopeful but sad-eyed men gathering around a mast erected by the roadside. Behind them women leaned exhausted on sheaves of dried corn in fields already ploughed for the winter.

Mirsad Duratovic's office did not have a computer, but he hoped for a miracle and then the telephone would give him internet connection.

'Biscani was raised to the ground,' he told us and explained his job as village representative: 'We have very limited help. We look for prospective donors to help us keep records, statistics, and to cooperate with agencies, issuing certificates when they are needed, vouching for returnees who have found donors, keeping in contact with institutions like the police. My office is the first place people turn to with problems. I liaise with officials on health, water and electricity issues and help provide these facilities that were cut off in the war. We ring up and press for results. Before the war there were three hundred and eighty eight households, and now two hundred and forty households are returning and rebuilding. Half the support comes from donors; families supply the other half themselves. Those who invested while living abroad and earning tend to stay abroad with their families. A hundred and four families are permanently residing here. Others come for summer holidays and help reconstruct villages and mosques. There is just one mosque in this village, no Orthodox or Catholic churches, not even before the war. We were always Bosniak. Serbs looted every-thing before destroying the homes, even selling cables, furniture etc. They made a fortune out of trading with Serbia what they stole. They even looted public property, which was after all for their use too, mining the railroad, ripping up materials and selling them as scrap, even tearing down their own school. A charity has now rebuilt the school.'

'When we returned we accepted that we had to reconcile with our neighbours,' Mirsad Duratovic continued. 'We don't have central heating but get wood from Serb villages, pay for it and they deliver. A businessman from Prijedor donated one thousand Bosnian marks for the mosque. A returnee from Germany is employed by Serbs to help mill wheat for flour. We Bosniaks also employ Serbs: our accountant is a Serb. There is cooperation between businesses and good neighbourly relations. But only as regards business.'

'The question of justice is something else though,' he said, at last focusing on the main issue. 'Do we have the patience to wait? When will we ever get justice? One thousand and five hundred people were murdered in a day here. No one has been indicted, arrested or charged with this murder. The Hague Tribunal has no interest in this region. There are still too many missing bodies. Ten of my close family members disappeared and no bones have been found yet. The war cannot stop until I find their remains. One of the drivers who took the bodies to mass graves still works in a firm in Prijedor. I used to have good personal contact with him before the war and invited him to Biscani. I took him to my house, though he did not realize then that I knew he had been a driver. I wanted to observe his behaviour. I know him, I know where he lives. Will I be able to resist doing something stupid?'

'In 1992 a cousin returned from the States with his wife,' he continued. 'It happened to be on the day of ethnic cleansing. A soldier from a neighbouring village cut his throat. I recently went and stood on the exact spot. At that moment this same soldier who killed him drove past me in a car. How long can we wait? It is such a huge inner struggle! Three sons of my grandmother were murdered. DNA identified two of them at Sejkovac. My grandfather died before finding out. But now my grandmother is ill with distress.'

When we returned the following month, Mirsad Duratovic invited us to meet his wife, aunt, grandmother and two sons. He showed us the woods where his uncles and brothers were taken and shot. Relations between the communities had now broken down. The Serbs in the neighbouring village, we could see it across the valley, had a week earlier blown up the bridge that connected Biscani with its cornfields, and Bosniaks from Biscani wanted to blow up another bridge in order to inconvenience the Serbs. Mirsad stopped them. 'We cannot continue the war. We have to find a way of living together in peace. I am not talking of reconciliation. There is still no justice for that. But we have to cooperate, and we must not allow ourselves to enter the vicious circle of revenge and counter-revenge. It is hard for us while we still look for the bodies of family that disappeared, and when we keep meeting everyday on our streets those who committed the murders. They drive past us without a care in the world. They destroyed our houses and cut down orchards and the woods. They knew we would return and wanted us to have nothing. The woods are growing as you can see, and we are planting new fruit trees, cultivating the land. We have one cow, and hopefully will afford to buy another; we sell milk and cheese.'

Mirsad Duratovic's grandmother lay on a hard bed suffering from pneumonia, her frail arms clinging to a light blanket and looking at us with sorrow beyond words and tears. Mirsad's wife graciously served us home-made cheese, coffee and almond cakes.

His son ran outside with a friend, brandishing bits of wood like swords. Mirsad discouraged them from playing with toy guns.

'I do not want to bring them up to be soldiers,' he told us. 'War and killing is not the way anymore. We have to learn to live in peace with each other.'

REMEMBERING FOR TOMORROW

Snow and rain fell over Bosnia when we returned for the conference and presentation. Birds of prey perched sentinel by muddy fields.

Representatives from the mine owners' head offices in Holland and London flew in to help with last minute hitches, encourage the mine management not to waver in their support for the project and observe the final stages of the mediation process.

'Hold to the process,' Graham Day told us and quoted Ivo Andric's observations about the mean-spiritness of Bosnians towards each other, a case of 'fuck your neighbour' rather than 'care for your neighbour'. Working for the United Nations in East Timor he had come across a tradition which allowed all parties to speak as much as they wanted, for however long, uninterrupted in the presence of community elders, all seated under the village tree. Such letting off steam helped prevent escalation of violence.

'Are they sincere?' Rezak Hukanovic wanted to know of the mine owners' representatives. 'They are the legal heirs of the old mines. As a citizen of this town of Prijedor I think the time of metaphysics is behind us. That they are still employing the man who was mine manager during the war gives cause for serious doubts. We have to name the mayor at the conference, as being against the project.'

'I have no problem speaking my mind,' said Muharem Murselovic. 'The future of the region is at stake. We have to describe the full horror of what happened. We have to be subtle and find experts to make the best job of the memorial possible. We must also listen to lots of people, the experts must listen also. As to the Bosniaks criticising from the diaspora, they have to live and work here. Then they will have the moral authority to take part.' He was referring to lengthy text messages from Sadko Mujagic in Rotterdam, and email letters that Sadko insisted on being read out at the conference.

'I talk with Rezak often and we both detect fear,' he went on.

'We put ourselves on the line all the time. These people speak from afar, talking to us from their comfortable homes and well-paid jobs suggesting what should happen. Despite my brusque manner I have had no problems with Serbs so far, only with Bosniaks, back stabbing and talking behind my back. It is a Bosniak mind-set. You can read it in the books of Ivo Andric and Mesa Selimovic. Selimovic tells a story: a man is about to be stoned to death. He is thinking about who will throw the first and the biggest stone. It will not be the man he never helped, but the one he helped most. It is a strange mentality.'

This reminded us of two words that sum up the paradoxical nature of Bosnia. On the one hand there is the tradition of *moba*, where people help build each other's homes, all hands together, especially after a marriage, friends bringing food and drink for the day and everyone taking part like the Amish community's barn-raising in Peter Weir's film, *The Witness*. Then there is *inat* – a tradition of mean-spirited nastiness Graham Day warned us about.

Edin Ramulic had given an interview to a local paper attacking the project, saying Bosniaks should have nothing to do with it. He tried to inject dissent into the process and undermine the presentation, but Muharem Murselovic said scornfully: 'He keeps saying he would like to shoot any Serbs who come to Sanski Most. It would be braver to shoot them here in Prijedor. We could never run out of them here!'

Emsuda Mujagic, 'a woman of modest intelligence' according to Rezak Hukanovic and Muharem Murselovic, gave a more sympathetic response. She and Nusreta Sivac constantly attempted to bring Edin Ramulic on board the project. 'He feels left out,' she told us. 'But he doesn't realize he is to blame. When we are not there for him he goes to pieces. He can't suppress his negativity. People wind him up. He over-reacts to what people say. Like the rest of the diaspora he is locked into his trauma and can only think in terms of of black and white, and retribution. He cannot see any place for reconciliation. Victims have to be the first to heal.'

She proposed that the diaspora be brought in after the conference. Sadko Mujagic, who kept texting and phoning us from

Rotterdam, was her son. He meant well and always tried to please everybody, however impossible, as he now tried to do with the project and those passionately opposed to it.

She incidentally also met the man who had broken into the mine offices when Bosniaks visited Omarska in August. He had told her: 'I don't know why, but I couldn't control myself. Being there in 1992 I had to let off steam. As I was breaking the door I also felt I was breaking out of prison.'

Anel, unruffled as always, commented on Edin Ramulic's interview: 'He has now done his worst, without any effect. Don't worry about him.'

Anel and Zoran had managed to organize several well-attended meetings where all the participants discussed and agreed on a proposal for the memorial. They had found a video artist to create a simulation of the memorial for the presentation. Zoran's attention to detail meant that the presentation passed off without a hitch. The mine owners' representatives were impressed, but could only guess at the exceptional difficulties faced by these two young men, a Bosniak and a Serb, making a success of an event which challenged history and entrenched attitudes.

On the international stage presidents and prime ministers, with unlimited expense and state of the art security at their disposal might get leaders from opposite sides of a war to agree on words and shake hands in front of the world media. But to persuade people on the ground, vulnerable to attack from all sides in their daily lives, to discuss issues of guilt, justice and reconciliation while preparing a tangible memorial to mark a recent community trauma – that was a more difficult proposition.

Graham Day's efforts to keep the mayor in line were in vain. The mayor sent a public statement saying the conference had no authority and that he would not be attending. The mayor also organized a special session of the Municipal Assembly to prevent Azra Pasalic, the Speaker of the Assembly, and those Serb politicians involved in the project, from attending the presentation. Azra Pasalic, who had agreed to chair the presentation, faced him off in the corridor outside his office: 'I had this conference in my diary for months; I have no intention of missing it.' 'But you are the Speaker of the Assembly!' the mayor protested. 'Nothing will stop me going, and I will chair the presentation,' she retorted.

Azra Pasalic with Nusreta Sivac's help worked on an introduction to the presentation: 'We need a helping hand from our friends, you who are present from all over the world. Friendship is the future. Young people are the future. Crimes happened in 1992. Three thousand were murdered or disappeared, thirty thousand banished. In 1992 horrific crimes took place at Omarska. People were killed because they were of a different faith. The purpose of this conference is to pay tribute to them. A memorial will help the future of the citizens of Prijedor. 1992 will become a memory.'

'Some people might criticize,' explained Nusreta Sivac. 'We need to have all the facts and statistics at our fingertips.'

The mine director now found himself besieged by the local Serb press, scenting that the mine management were about to authorize a memorial. The mine owners' representatives hurried to the director's assistance and to show solidarity, that decisions about the memorial came from Holland and London, not only from the mine.

We met the mine director for our final meeting before the conference and he seemed calm. 'It is absolutely necessary to deal with this issue in the smoothest manner,' he told us. 'I talked with the mine owners' chief executive on the phone to see how we can steer the presentation in a good direction. There are people from both sides who oppose the project. Threats and criticisms come from both sides. This shows how difficult our task is. Whatever we do we will get criticism. We must blank out extreme views. We must not give the impression that we have reached a decision. Keep open so other people can join in later. It will be interesting to see how the memorial becomes self-sustaining. We will study the proposals and decide who will be in charge: the mine or the local community. In my opinion the mine should not be responsible for its upkeep. This memorial must mark something that happened, but that has nothing to do with the present mine. It will make my life easier to be dissociated.'

We reassured him that we planned to set up a management committee including a representative of the mine to deal specifically with issues of security and access.

THE PRESENTATION

On the evening of Wednesday 30th November the participants of the project gave a detailed presentation focusing on a proposal for the memorial at Omarska to the mine owners' representatives and guests from the international community including Graham Day from the Office of the High Representative. Mathew Lawson, head of the British Embassy office in Banja Luka, came with his Serb wife along with several women from Hearts for Peace, English and Bosnian.

This presentation served as a dress rehearsal for the press conference next morning. We planned to sharpen up the speeches for the second presentation, shortening that event to give time for questions. Afterwards we planned to take everybody, press included, by bus and convoy of cars to Omarska and the white house.

The presentations brought the second phase of the project to an end. The participants planned to form a management committee afterwards and work towards completion of the project, a memorial at Omarska.

Most of the participants turned up, including the three women from the mine management, despite harrassment from the Serb media in Prijedor and aware that the mayor had expressed disapproval. The older Serbs, Zeljko Kantar and Zarko Gvozden did not appear, and gave no explanation, but we assumed they were afraid. Nino Jauz, the mine director's wife and other politicians obeyed Mayor Pavic's orders to attend the Municipal Assembly session that he organized at the last minute to coincide with the presentation. Most of the young Serbs from Info Point and the 'round table' came. The exceptions were Sasha Drakulic who had already told us he wanted nothing more to do with the project, and Katerina Panic, the journalist, who had unwillingly to cover the Municipal Assembly session. Mirjana Verhabovic the only Croat among the participants could not come because her son had been suddenly taken to hospital with a heart attack. Despite these absences the most significant players were present, all those scheduled to speak and others including Mirsad Duratovic.

Anel and Zoran arranged for tight security around the Atina Hotel, and insisted that everyone, participants and guests, be given a formal welcome at the entrance. The four of us greeted all the participants and guests as they arrived.

At the afternoon rehearsal before the first presentation the speakers seemed stiff and formal, reading from scripts like school children, but in the evening everything went like clockwork.

Azra Pasalic, chairing the presentation, gave her introduction with a repetition of historic facts. Then the presentation focused on a technically smooth video presentation allowing the survivors Muharem Murselovic and Rezak Hukanovic respectively to give context and to describe the proposals for the memorial, followed by Boris Danovic explaining the lay-out of the mine, entrances and exits, space for car-parking and fencing off the memorial site. Rezak had wavered about attending and speaking, because of his suspicions about the mine owners' motives concerning the memorial. But he arrived, hunched, grim-faced and chain-smoking as usual. He spoke expansively about the significance of the white house, and explained the purpose of the memorial, the way it would look inside and outside the white house.

Some of the guests, though happy with the progress of the project and especially the well-organized conference, did not care for the appearance of the memorial with statues, paths, fountains and evergreens reminiscent of a suburban cemetery. We explained that these were part of a proposal which would be altered and refined in the next phase of the project, dedicated to implementing the conference's decisions, widening participation to include the diaspora and eventually overseeing the building of the memorial. Agreement between all sides on the basic necessity and lay out for a memorial mattered more at this stage.

To round off the first presentation the mine director pledged the mine's support for the project. Emsuda Mujagic and Nusreta

Sivac were given time to deliver long speeches. When they had finished talking about the need for peace and reconciliation, Rezak Hukanovic sneaked a despairing look at us and left the room.

Immediately after this first presentation Rezak Hukanovic received an uninterrupted string of calls on his mobile from a withheld number in Croatia, all of them death threats if he dared to repeat his talk at the press conference. He kept quiet about the calls until later in the evening, after a party in the Atina downstairs club bar, and most of the participants had gone to bed. Then he told Anel. They both realized that the first call happened immediately after he had spoken, which meant that one of the participants must have been in contact with the anonymous caller. At first they could not be sure if it was a Serb or Bosniak threat. It seemed to be Bosniak, because at this stage of the project the main criticism came from the diaspora. Serbs had already 'marked' the young Serbs from the 'round table' and Info Point, and were harrassing Rezak regularly. The mayor did not need to make this kind of threat. But which Bosniak at the conference would have informed the caller?

An emergency meeting was called with those of us still awake. We did not need to be too alarmed by the threat if Anel and Rezak could handle it. Anel had been receiving menacing calls and emails from Serb nationalist groups for months, and Rezak was also used to living with death threats, including a bomb exploding outside his home on our previous visit. We ourselves had also been warned off the project by Edin Ramulic and the diaspora.

Rezak Hukanovic decided to sleep on it, but planned to repeat his presentation at the press conference. We shortened the event, cutting out many speeches and allowing the representatives from Holland and London to speak on behalf of the mine although the mine director still intended to give his speech of support.

A high point of the project took place in the Atina club bar. At last everyone relaxed and sat together, no longer Serbs and Bosniaks in separate groups at different tables. Despite the phone threats Rezak Hukanovic showed no hint of stress, laughing and joking with the young Serbs from Info Point and the 'round table' who gathered around him their eyes glistening with admiration and respect. Just the sight of them all mixing and talking about the project in such good spirits momentarily made all efforts seem worthwhile. Whatever obstacles and disasters that would befall the project - and no one present underestimated these - at least the memory of this gathering remained.

The Atina hotel staff meanwhile converted the conference room back into a restaurant and everyone moved upstairs for a buffet supper.

The presenters realized the inadequacy of the memorial's appearance, and proposed that the mine owners establish a competition to find a sculptor and landscape designer to help turn the white house into a unique international monument. Graham Day insisted these should be Bosnian, even if it meant attracting back artists who had fled the country to carve out successful careers in securer and richer parts of the world. These issues would become the basis for the next workshop discussions after the conference. If we could not find Bosnian artists, we would bring professionals experienced in this kind of project, and work together with the locals.

'Do you honestly think there will be a memorial?' asked one of the women from the mine management, once again sitting separately from the other participants along with the other two mine women and Zoran Ergerac. We agreed with them that the most difficult part of the project would follow the conference, and were preparing for that by forming a management committee made up of the strongest and most resolute participants to carry the work forward.

Next morning at the press conference attended by local, national and international journalists the mine director spoke about the mine's support for a memorial. A headline in The Times reported: *Enemies to build horror camp memorial*. Afterwards we thanked him for his courage in the teeth of Serb opposition. 'It must have been difficult,' we said. 'Not difficult at all,' he said smiling and looking intently at us. 'It was easy.'

Snow fell over fields, woods and mountains as the convoy of coaches and cars transported the press corps, participants and guests to Omarska.

Serbs and Bosniaks wandered together over the mine complex and the fields around the white house.

Alison Rooper of In Focus Productions had asked two young people from Info Point to make a video record of the event so she could include it in her documentary. For the first time these Serb men felt able to enter the white house. They had a job to do, and pointed the camcorder in every corner and at all the people coming in and out.

Mirsad Duratovic took me to the empty shower room where as a terrified seventeen year old his hands and legs had been tied with ropes while they beat him. 'They made me crouch in the shower for hours,' he said. 'I expected to die.'

Visitors now crowded in all the rooms and Mirsad shot a dagger glance at Muharem Murselovic and the mine director talking animatedly in the entrance. 'This is no place for politics,' Mirsad hissed to me. For the first time I saw this gentle man angry.

At that moment we both realized that the white house as a memorial required restricted access, and a mood of respect. There must not be chatter. The memorial had to be about reflection, meditation and silence.

Outside, the media interviewed participants and security officers from the mine looked on with friendly smiles. Six months earlier no one had dared look at the white house. Now people swarmed all over it.

Snow fell more heavily and people began to leave.

As they entered the coaches Boris Danovic approached one survivor after another to shake their hands and thank them for allowing him to be part of the project. Emsuda Mujagic and Nusreta Sivac looked surprised but took his hand. A small gesture but it reminded us of a saying by Desmond Tutu: 'Never underestimate the importance of a handshake.'

We received a mobile phone text in German from Mirsad Duratovic next day as we drove to Zagreb airport on our way home. A dark grey winter sky lowered over snow-streaked muddy fields.

The text said: 'I arrived home safely. My friends are saying that it is almost unimaginable what we achieved. The struggle continues. Mirso'

AFTERWORD

Not desiring the fruits of action. For us there is only the trying, the rest is not our business.
TS Eliot

Following the conference we continued the search for artists and designers.

Our deadline was May 2006 by which time the outline for the memorial would have to have been acceptable to the Omarska survivors, the mine management and the municipality of Prijedor.

The Soul of Europe was fully aware of the difficulties of getting agreement, but given our painstaking and thorough preparation we knew we could bring people together to reach an acceptable solution.

Then in February 2006 we received a message that the project had been put 'on hold'.

There was concern about the serious disagreements within the Bosniak communities particularly between survivors who had returned to Prijedor and those from the diaspora.

However, the newly created management group of Omarska survivors from Prijedor had begun to address this problem.

This decision to put the project 'on hold' was hard for the Soul of Europe. We had spent months bringing Serbs and Bosniaks together. They were now talking together. The Soul of Europe had gained their trust. It would not have been impossible to bring Mayor Marko Pavic to put up with the memorial even as he distanced himself from it.

Though the project was disrupted, our relationships with all the participants remained firm. Our Bosniak friends were stoical: 'What else do you expect from Europe?'

A Survivors of Omarska Committee has been established under the presidency of Mirsad Duratovic, and they are taking the project further.

Katerina Panic, the Serb journalist from the 'round table' told me in June 2006: 'The memorial can only progress on the foundations of the work you have laid down.'